Should You RUN!
From *Jesus Always?*
A Revealing Look at the *Jesus Always* Devotional.

Steven Hudgik

Copyright © 2016, 2017 Steven Hudgik
Abridged Edition

All rights reserved. No part of this publication may be reproduced, distributed, or transmitted in any form or by any means, including photocopying, recording, or other electronic or mechanical methods, without the prior written permission of the publisher, except in the case of brief quotations embodied in critical reviews and certain other noncommercial uses permitted by copyright law. For permission requests, write to the author at the following address:

Move to Assurance
P.O. Box 277
Cannon Beach, OR 97110

ISBN-10: 153985583X
ISBN-13: 978-1539855835

SOURCES OF SCRIPTURE QUOTATIONS

Unless otherwise noted, scripture is taken from the NEW AMERICAN STANDARD BIBLE, copyright © 1960, 1963, 1968, 1971, 1972, 1973, 1975, 1977, 1995 by The Lockman Foundation. Used by permission.

Because other translations are used by *Jesus Always*, there are times when I must quote from those translations When the NKJV has been used it is indicated by the NKJV abbreviation: NKJV - Scripture taken from the New King James Version®. Copyright © 1982 by Thomas Nelson. Used by permission. All rights reserved. | When The Message is quoted, those quotes are indicated by the abbreviation MSG. – The Message is copyright by Eugene H. Peterson 1993, 1994, 1995, 1996, 2000, 2001, 2002. Used by permission of Tyndale House Publishers, Inc. | When the NIV is quoted it is indicated by "NIV." – The NIV is copyright 1973, 1978, 1984 Used by permission of Zondervan. All rights reserved worldwide. www.zondervan.com.

DEDICATION

A number of people have given their time to help at Cannon Beach Bible Church, with the ministries of Move to Assurance, and in our personal life. They have given what is most precious, their time, to help knock aside the many distractions Satan has thrown in my path. Some have some raked leaves and split firewood, some hauled away many loads of trash and debris, others have filled the pulpit, and many have prayed for us. Without their help this book would not have been written. I want to express my deepness appreciation and gratitude to Bill & Marsha, Aaron & Heather, John & Jody, Wade & Connie, Bob Brown, SWHBC, the entire Fies family, Mike, Matthew, Kristen, Peter, Aaron, Nathan, Ryan and Felecia for all you have done to help my wife and I deal with all that has come at us in the past year. Thank you, I dedicate this book to you.
THANK YOU VERY MUCH!

This is an abridged version of the book: *"Sarah Young's Jesus Always Devotional EXPOSED!"*

THANK YOU

My sincere thanks to two people who, by reading and commenting on an early draft, helped to make this a much better book. Thank you Wendi McCloy and Dale Thompson! Your feedback, questions, and comments were gratefully accepted and very welcome. I can't tell you how much I appreciate all of the hours you put into reading and sharing your thoughts. Thank you!

I also wish to thank Warren Smith for his help. He patiently answered questions and helped me to be better understand New Age teaching and practices.

...holding fast the faithful word which is in accordance with the teaching, so that he will be able both to exhort in sound doctrine and to refute those who contradict.

Titus 1:9

CONTENTS

	Introduction	1
1	Test Yourself & Test *Jesus Always*	9
2	I Read *Jesus* Always And…	13
3	Why RUN From *Jesus Always*?	17
4	Why Doesn't Jesus Understand What He Said In Scripture? -- Matthew 24:4-25:30	25
5	Spotting New Age Teaching	35
6	Why Doesn't Jesus Understand Psalm 46?	41
7	Break Time	49
8	My Presence – What Does This Mean?	51
9	The True Presence of Jesus	59
10	What Keeps Us From God's Presence?	67
11	Why Doesn't Jesus Understand Scripture? May 29th	**75**
12	True Joy: What Does Scripture Say?	83
13	True Joy: The Source Of A Believer's Joy	95
14	Depression & The Fruit of The Spirit	99
16	Jesus Speaking: Sinful or Acceptable?	107
17	Jesus Speaking Makes the Book More Interesting	113
18	But, *Jesus Always* Really Helped Me	117
19	Trusting The Real Jesus To Heal You:	123
20	Should You RUN From Jesus Always?	127
	About the Author	131

Now the Spirit expressly says that in later times some will depart from the faith by devoting themselves to deceitful spirits and teachings of demons…

―

1 Timothy 4:

MAY GOD BE GLORIFIED

My desire is that God is glorified through this book. I pray that people will come to know the real Jesus, the Son of God, and not be lead astray by the false Jesus of *Jesus Always*.

I am grateful to our Lord Jesus Christ. Without His saving work on the cross all of humanity would be doomed and there would be no purpose nor point to anything. And thank you to the Holy Spirit for the gifts of the spirit. Without the peace and joy from the Holy Spirit, getting through the many and significant distractions and roadblocks to writing this book would have been impossible. And thank you to the Father for making this all possible. May God be glorified through this book and through those who using this book for witnessing and teaching.

> *…we have not ceased to pray for you and to ask that you may be filled with the knowledge of His will in all spiritual wisdom and understanding, so that you will walk in a manner worthy of the Lord, to please Him in all respects, bearing fruit in every good work and increasing in the knowledge of God; strengthened with all power, according to His glorious might, for the attaining of all steadfastness and patience; joyously giving thanks to the Father, who has qualified us to share in the inheritance of the saints in Light.* – Paul's prayer for the Colossians, Colossians 1:9-12

ALL GLORY TO GOD!!

Discernment is not a matter of simply telling the difference between what is right and wrong; rather, it is the difference between right and almost right.

C.H. Spurgeon

INTRODUCTION

INTRODUCTION

Beloved, do not believe every spirit, but test the spirits to see whether they are from God, because many false prophets have gone out into the world.
- 1 John 4:1

Beware of false prophets, who come to you in sheep's clothing but inwardly are ravenous wolves. – Matthew 7:15

Now these were more noble-minded than those in Thessalonica, for they received the word with great eagerness, examining the Scriptures daily to see whether these things were so. – Acts 17:11

In 2015 I wrote a book called *"RUN, It's Jesus Calling"* warning about the unbiblical nature of Sarah Young's *Jesus Calling* devotional book. In October 2016 a new devotional book by Sarah Young was released, *Jesus Always, Embracing JOY in His Presence."* It retains the New Age mystical messages of the original book, but does more to hide them within Christian words, phrases, and beliefs. The abundance of Christian-speak serves as camouflage and the unsuspecting are unknowingly introduced to unbiblical practices and false teaching disguised as Christian truth.

When an enemy is seen for what he is, we are alerted and can be prepared to defend ourselves. But when an enemy poses as a friend, our defenses are down.
– John MacArthur, New Testament Commentary Matthew 1-7, 1985, page 464

"New Age Mystical Messages? What Are They?

Also known as the New Spirituality, New Gospel or the New Worldview, New Age is a buffet of beliefs drawn from a variety of sources, with an emphasis on the practices of Eastern religions. Many of these beliefs and practices are becoming embedded in the Christian church.

Some of the characteristics New Age include having direct personal spiritual experiences (experience validates truth); believing god is "within you and all life is connected spiritually; a focus on feelings instead of Biblical knowledge; and discernment is rarely mentioned. New Age spirituality involves practices such as: contemplative prayer, yoga, practicing the Presence, silence, mantras or short repetitious prayers, meditation, mandalas, and mindfulness.

In this book I'll cover some of the New Age aspects of *Jesus Always*, but my main focus will be on Biblical truth. I'll reveal the "poison" in *Jesus Always* by showing that it is teaching Biblical truth. If you'd like to learn more about New Age spirituality, I recommend Ray Yungen's book, *"A Time Of Departing."* Or visit my web site at: www.NOTJesusAlways.com

Why Am I Writing This Book?

I recognize my saying a book is unbiblical does not mean it is actually unbiblical. In addition, maybe I have selfish motives for writing this book. For example, I be looking to build my reputation or maybe even become famous. Or possibly I'm thinking this book will bring in huge royalty payments and I'll get rich quick.

None of those are true. My motive is a passion for Biblical truth and God's glory. My desire is that no one be led away from the true Jesus Christ, nor the truth of scripture, by a deceptive New Age book such as *Jesus Always*. But how can you know this is true? It is the same motive I had for writing *RUN! It's Jesus Calling*. For example:

- To date I have given away at least four times as many copies of *RUN! It's Jesus Calling* than have been sold. For example, anyone coming to our church (being in a tourist town we have lots of visitors) may pick up a free copy from our literature table. To the extent I can afford it, I plan to do the same with this book.

- All of the royalties from my books go directly to a non-profit ministry.

- I typically do not do speaking engagements. I am currently serving as a missionary planting a church in Cannon Beach, Oregon. That is my primary calling.

So, what other possible motives could I have? Love. I don't know you, but I love you and care about you. And I love Jesus and the truth. And that means doing what Jesus did – speaking the truth.

What Was Jesus' #1 Priority?

Jesus' #1 priority is that you be saved

The Lord is not slow about His promise, as some count slowness, but is patient toward you, not wishing for any to perish but for all to come to repentance. – 2 Peter 3:9

Jesus is love. Jesus loves everyone, including the Pharisees and scribes whom He condemned as vipers and white-washed tombs (Matthew 23:27). So what did He do? He spoke the truth to them. His greatest concern is for as many as possible to be saved from the wrath of God (hell), including Pharisees. They only way for that to happen is to speak the truth. Lies cannot save you.

For even the Son of Man did not come to be served, but to serve, and to give His life a ransom for many. – Mark 10:45

It is a trustworthy statement, deserving full acceptance that Christ Jesus came into the world to save sinners… - 1 Timothy 1:15

I will demonstrate that the "Jesus" of *Jesus Always* is not the real Jesus. For example, he changes the meaning of scripture, he is not discerning (not able to separate the true from the false), and he presents unbiblical New Age teaching. To follow the teaching of *Jesus*

Always is to follow a lie… a false Jesus. It is taking the broad road to destruction (see Matthew 7:13-14). My purpose is to do as Jesus did, speak the truth in love. I am sounding a warning (Ezekiel 33:1-6) about an unbiblical book that claims to be a Christian devotional.

Jesus Always – A Wolf in Sheep's Clothing

Jesus Always is a devotional that poses as a Christian book… it poses as a "shepherd" guiding Christians in the practices that promise to help them feel "closer" to Jesus. But, like Sarah Young's first book, *Jesus Calling*, it is a white-washed tomb – it sounds good on the surface, but inside it is filled with death.

Jesus Calling, had many obvious problems, such as Jesus saying things that directly contradict scripture; Jesus not understanding scripture; and Jesus promoting a New Age agenda. In *Jesus Always* it is obvious that significant effort has gone into making those types of errors harder to detect. For example, *Jesus Always* uses an abundance of Christian phrases and terms. It talks about sin, the cross, repentance, and Biblical practices such as reading scripture. The Jesus of *Jesus Always* even refers to himself as "your Savior" and he "quotes" scripture frequently.

But the truth about *Jesus Always* comes out when you examine what this "Jesus" actually says and compare it with scripture. In many cases he doesn't even understand what scripture is saying. He is nothing more than a poor caricature of the real Jesus. The *Jesus Always* devotion has the appearance of an angel of light, but it carries readers away from the true Jesus and toward unbiblical beliefs and practices.

> *The false shepherd (the deceiver) gives the appearance of orthodoxy, frequently with great declarations and fanfare. He is not a liberal or a cultist but one who speaks favorably of Christ, the cross, the Bible, the Holy Spirit, and so on, and who associates with true believers.* – John MacArthur, New Testament Commentary Matthew 1-7, 1985, page 464

> *For such men are false apostles, deceitful workers, disguising themselves as apostles of Christ. No wonder, for even Satan disguises himself as an angel of light.* – 2 Corinthians 11:13-14

INTRODUCTION

> *How then can we describe these people? What is wrong with their teaching? ...It is a teaching, the falseness of which is to be detected by what it does not say rather than by what it does say. And it is at this point that we realize the subtlety of the situation.* – D. Martyn Lloyd-Jones, Studies in the Sermon on the Mount, 1976, page 500

Anyone can create a fictional character and name that character "Jesus." They can even claim that fictional character is the Jesus of the bible. But it is still just fiction. If you put your trust in a fictional character, what do you have? Nothing. If you put your trust in a fictional character to give you the truth, what do you have? Nothing.

That's what you get in the *Jesus Always* devotional. A fictional Jesus who gives you a false sense of peace and joy.

But, it feels good, you say? How can it be false? New Age practices do have real effects. They can produce real feelings of joy and peace. BUT... because these feelings do not come from the true Jesus, they are not the truth and they don't last. And that is a big problem.

> *An amazing thing is happening across the land. Jesus Christ is being "reinvented" and redefined right in front of our eyes and hardly anyone seems to notice or care. And it is happening with great speed. The "transformational" architects and promoters of a New Age/New Gospel are unabashedly trying to overturn God's holy Word and replace the true Christ—Jesus Christ—with a false Christ of Antichrist proportions.* – Warren Smith, False Christ Coming, 2011, page 15

What is the Source of Biblical Joy?

As Sarah Young's subtitle states, *Jesus Always* is about *"Embracing Joy in His Presence."* So some key questions are: Why do we have joy? Where does our joy come from?

It comes from the cross of Christ. We have joy because of the cross. Because of the cross we have salvation and a promise of eternal life. Because of the cross we have the indwelling of the Holy Spirit who gives us joy as one of the fruits of having the Spirit.

> *Joy is that Spirit-produced virtue which enables the believer to rejoice in all the circumstances of life. Even in trials, the believer may retain the joy of the Lord which prevents his giving way to total despair.* – The Freedom of

God's Sons, Studies in Galatians, Homer A. Kent, Jr., 1976, page 161

True joy is a gift from God to those who believe the gospel, being produced in them by the Holy Spirit as they receive and obey the Word, mixed with trials, and set their hope on future glory. – John MacArthur, The Epistle of Joy, sermon available online at: http://tinyurl.com/zm2ukn8

True joy results from salvation, the indwelling of the Holy Spirit, obeying God's word, and experiencing trials. If you are not saved... if you are not a true Christian following the real Jesus, you do not have true joy.

That's my motive. I want you to know the real Jesus. The Jesus of scripture who came to earth to seek and save the lost... to seek and save you. That's what this book is about... having the completeness of joy that comes from the real Jesus knowing you.

What If You Have Never Heard of *Jesus Always*?

First, stay away from it. Don't read it. Don't buy a copy. If someone gives you a copy, throw it away.

Second, I think you'll still find this book useful. It not only reveals the unbiblical nature of *Jesus Always*, it also reveals the real Jesus and what it means to truly be in His presence. AND, it will show you how to have real joy... a joy that your circumstances cannot take away. And finally, it will teach you how to spot false teaching. I don't just say that *Jesus Always* is unbiblical, I'll show you why it is unbiblical, and I'll teach you principles you can apply to uncover similar false teachers and unbiblical teaching.

The only way to understand rightly this picture of false prophets... He [the false teacher] has nothing which is offensive to the natural man; he pleases all. He is in "sheep's clothing," so attractive, so pleasant, so nice ton look at. He has such a nice and comfortable and comforting message. – D. Martyn Lloyd Jones, Studies in the Sermon on the Mount, 1976, pages 500-501

INTRODUCTION

A Final Note

To keep the original book (*Jesus Always EXPOSED*) to a reasonable length (about 220 pages) I did not included everything I could have included. To make the book you are now reading an even quicker read, it includes only the most important scriptural comparisons and tests that demonstrate the unbiblical nature of *Jesus Always* If you'd like more information, including videos and articles about New Age practices and spirituality, go to my web web site at: www.NotJesusAlways.com.

In addition, I have written another book that makes a good companion for this book. It lays out the Biblical path to true joy as described by Jesus in the Beatitudes. That book is called "*Happy Are The…*" It is available on the web site (www.NotJesusAlways.com) and on Amazon.

SHOULD YOU RUN FROM *JESUS ALWAYS*?

CHAPTER 1
TEST YOURSELF & TEST *JESUS ALWAYS*

This book is about obeying God's commands concerning testing teaching and testing yourself. Obedience and love are based on having discernment. You cannot obey God, unless you are following true teaching. And you cannot truly love, unless you are obeying God.

Why do we need to test ourselves? I'm guessing most of you are Christians. Why? Because you are following the Biblical command to test the spirits… you are reading this book to learn how to test *Jesus Always*. Most of the people who have written to me about my book *"RUN! It's Jesus Calling"* have started out by saying, *"A friend gave me a copy of Jesus Calling and as I read it I could tell something was wrong, but I wasn't sure what it was."* They were believers and immediately knew that Sarah Young's first devotional, *Jesus Calling*, was not a Biblical devotional.

However, the church includes many people who believe they are Christians, but are not. I'm not saying this to be mean or to hurt your feelings. It is a fact in scripture that is plainly taught by Jesus. It is a fact all Christians know and accept. Jesus used an example of wheat and tares:

> *Jesus presented another parable to them, saying, "The kingdom of heaven may be compared to a man who sowed good seed in his field. But while his men were sleeping, his enemy came and sowed tares* [weeds that look exactly like wheat] *among the wheat, and went away. But when the wheat sprouted and bore grain, then the tares became evident also.* – Matthew 13:24-26

Tares look exactly like wheat. When wheat and tares are growing in the same field, you can't tell one from the other. Only at harvest time does the difference become apparent.

Jesus is saying there are false Christians (tares) among the true Christians in the church (the wheat), and you can't always tell them apart. In fact, even the false Christians do not know they are false Christians:

Many will say to Me on that day, 'Lord, Lord, did we not prophesy in Your name, and in Your name cast out demons, and in Your name perform many miracles?' And then I will declare to them, "I never knew you; depart from Me, you who practice lawlessness." – Matthew 7:22-23

Notice in the above scripture that false Christians can have a solid assurance of their "faith." And they can be doing many things that validate them as Christians. They're helping other people, serving in the church, and doing all sorts of good works. But the reality is that... Jesus does not know them.

And notice there are not just a few of these people. Jesus begins Matthew 22:7 with the word "many." There will be **many** people who believe they are truly Christians when in fact they are not. This is a disturbing statement. But these are the words of scripture, so they are true.

What about you? How can you know you truly are a believer? Is it because you feel you are a Christian? Is it because you were born into a Christian family? Is it because you've always been a Christian? None of these are indicators that someone is a Christian. Being a Christian isn't a feeling, nor is it something that can be passed on to us by our parents.

So what are we to do? We are commanded to test ourselves to see if we are in the faith. This is not a suggestion nor a recommendation. It is a command from God, test yourself!

Test yourselves to see if you are in the faith; examine yourselves! Or do you not recognize this about yourselves; that Jesus Christ is in you—unless indeed you fail the test? – 2 Corinthians 13:5

We are fallen creatures and we are easily deceived. Because your salvation is so important, and God does not want any of you to be lost, scripture commands you to test yourself. As you read this book you will learn a number of ways to test yourself.

What Else Does Scripture Tell You to Test?

Beloved, do not believe every spirit, but test the spirits to see whether they are from God, because many false prophets have gone out into the world. – 1 John 4:1

You are to test books such as *Jesus Always*. Is the teaching in *Jesus Always* in accordance with scripture? John is warning you that MANY false prophets are out there attempting to mislead you. There's that word "many" again. This is not a small problem.

So test before you trust. If what *Jesus Always* teaches is not in agreement with scripture, Sarah Young is a false teacher and you should avoid her books.

What about this book? Test it! Is what I say biblical? Am I accurately representing what scripture says? Test this book against scripture.

Scripture commands us to test ourselves and test what others are teaching. This is not optional. It is a command in scripture… a command from God. To disobey this command is to practice lawlessness, a sign you are not saved (Matthew 7:22-23).

All through the New Testament we see Christians testing, praying, and approving. All manner of matters of life and faith are tested. Any teaching to which we are introduced is to be tested. Any decision we face is to be tested. There should be no belief, no teaching, no action in the life of the Christian or in the church that has not been thoroughly tested or scrutinized. – Tim Challies, The Discipline of Spiritual Discernment, 2007, pages 84 & 85

SHOULD YOU RUN FROM *JESUS ALWAYS*?

CHAPTER 2
I READ *JESUS ALWAYS* AND...

As I read *Jesus Always* it was obvious considerable effort had gone into addressing the problems books such as Warren Smith's "*Another Jesus Calling*" and my *"RUN! It's Jesus Calling"* had revealed. For example, *Jesus Always* includes a huge amount of "scripture." Not only does every devotion have three or four scripture references, but Jesus quotes "scripture" in nearly every devotion. These quotes are put in italics so we can easily see where Jesus is quoting from scripture.

"Jesus" also encourages his readers to be in scripture and to be living in obedience to his will. He talks about sin and the cross. He states that he is the savior, and in a few devotions he declares he is the only savior and even proclaims the gospel.

So what's wrong? If it has all of these Biblical characteristics, why am I wasting time writing this book? Is it because I hate Sarah Young and want to attack her no matter what she writes? No. I'm writing this book because I love the true Jesus as well as Sarah Young. And while she has included the "gospel" in *Jesus Always,* it also includes deadly poison

The Big Bowl of Skittles

My favorite radio program is an internet show called Wretched. A few weeks ago the host, Todd Friel, gave an example that perfectly illustrates the problem with *Jesus Always*.

SHOULD YOU RUN FROM *JESUS ALWAYS*?

Imagine you have a big bowl Skittles candies. You love Skittles, but, someone has put a poison pill in that bowl. To eat that poison brings certain death.

The poison pill looks similar to a Skittle. You can tell them apart, but only if you look closely. You want to enjoy the wonderful flavors of those Skittles, so what are you going to do? Will you:

A) Grab handfuls of Skittles from the bowl and gulp them down, enjoying the pleasure of eating Skittles.

B) Will you slowly inspect each Skittle before you eat it, hoping to spot the poison?

C) Will you dump the bowl down the toilet, go to the store, buy more Skittles, and then enjoy these pure Skittles with no fear of poison?

Most people who read *Jesus Always* have already chosen option "A," simply because they don't know about the poison. You know better. You have knowledge they don't have. So if you pick anything other than option "C," you are not making a wise choice.

Now imagine it's worse than you thought. Many of the Skittles have been injected with poison. The bowl has more poison than it has pure Skittles. Some of the poison is easy to spot, but some of the poison Skittles look very much like pure, clean Skittles. Are you going to take a chance and eat from the bowl? No way!

This second analogy is the more accurate description of Sarah Young's *Jesus Always*. It includes some scriptural truth, but there is a lot of poison. Some of it is easy to spot, but a lot of the poison is difficult to spot. Are you willing to feed your soul from this book?

Discernment is not simply a matter of telling the difference between what is right and wrong; rather it is the difference between right and almost right. – Charles Spurgeon

No sane person will eat food when there is even a small risk of that food being contaminated with poison. I hope you are not willing to eat spiritual food, when there is a risk of poisoning your soul.

So What Is The Problem With *Jesus Always*?

That's what this book is about, and I'll provide scriptural proof of what I say. To give you a quick preview, here are two major issues:

> *1. Jesus Always* presents a false Jesus who cannot save you, nor can he sanctify you. The "Jesus" of *Jesus Always* does not even correctly understand scripture! He's just another false Christ. The real Jesus, in Matthew 7, warns about false teachers and prophets, as does John in 2 John:
>
> *Beware of the false prophets, who come to you in sheep's clothing, but inwardly are ravenous wolves.* Matthew 7:15
>
> *For many deceivers have gone out into the world.* – 2 John 7
>
> As you read this book you will learn, from scripture, why the Jesus of *Jesus Always* is a false Jesus who is leading his readers away from the truth.
>
> *2. Jesus Always* is a gateway that introduces its readers to a false New Age type of religion. The Jesus of *Jesus Always* straight out says that he is training you. What is he training you to do? To believe in and use New Age spiritual practices such as Presence, silence, contemplative (repetitious) prayer, and believing that god is in everything. I'll explain these as we go along.
>
> The most common New Age practice in *Jesus Always* is that of the "Presence" of Jesus, and it is definitely not biblical. Since it is a major theme in *Jesus Always*, I plan to spend quite a bit of time on this. To get us started, here is a quick comparison:
>
> **New Age:** everyone has god within them and as a part of them. By practicing such disciplines as silence, repetitive prayers, mindfulness, and living in the present (the now), you can become aware of god's Presence within you and be guided (taught) by him.

The Bible: God is separate from us, but active in our lives. While the Holy Spirit dwells within believers, He is not a part of us. We don't come into God's presence, we know is active (He is present) by seeing the results of God working in and through our lives.

Jesus Always Is Filled with Scripture, it has to be Biblical.

Quoting scripture does not make a book, nor a person Biblical. False teachers love to quote scripture (frequently out of context). Yes—even Satan quotes scripture! (Matthew 4:6) Quoting scripture helps to hide their false teaching.

If you look at the devotions in *Jesus Always* notice the words in italics. Those are quotes from scripture. Typically (but not always) the quote is from one of the verses identified at the bottom of the page.

However, when this "Jesus" quotes scripture, he does not always quote it. Instead he paraphrases it, and sometimes his "quote" is a paraphrase of a paraphrase. That can change the meaning of the scripture and it makes it harder to identify the source of the quote and read it in context. But what is really strange is that sometimes "Jesus" quotes just single words, such as the words "*all,*" "*either,*" (September 25th) and "*when*" (June 17th). That is simply absurd

I recommend reading a page in *Jesus Always* you most likely skipped. It's the page that lists the Bible translations used for the quotes from scripture. Be wary any time you see large numbers of translations referenced, such as you'll see here. That usually means the author is picking and choosing the "translation" that makes scripture say what the author wants it to say. *Jesus Always* quotes from fourteen different translations. That's a bad sign.

In addition, look at the quality of the translations. *Jesus Always* uses some excellent translations such as the KJV, NKJV and the NASB. But, it also uses some problem translations such as The Message and the Good News Bible.

Are there red warning lights and sirens starting to go off in your head? I hope so. The *Jesus Always* devotional has problems. But we haven't even started yet.

CHAPTER 3
WHY RUN FROM *JESUS ALWAYS*?

I'm not a fan of rap music, but every now and then I run across a Christian rap song that catches my attention. In a song about false teachers Shai Linne raps:

> *And you're thinking they're not the dangerous type*
> *'Cause some of their statements are right?*
> *That only proves that Satan comes as an angel of light.*
> - from the song Fal$e Teacher$

Satan comes as an angel of light. He hides the darkness of his true nature with the appearance of an angel of light. False teachers hide their false teaching in truth. In some cases what they teach may be 99.9% pure. But, that small 0.1% portion of poison can kill you. For example, a gallon of water with just 0.03% polonium 210 (much less than 0.1%) is poisonous enough to kill 10 million people. One teaspoon of botulinum toxin is more than enough to kill everyone in the U.S.. And false teachers are even more dangerous.

> *The invasion of false prophets, false teachers, false apostles, false Christs has been something which the people of God have endured through all the ages of time. Satan attempts to oversow the truth with lies. He attempts to confuse the world so that they cannot perceive the truth of God by drowning them in a sea of deceit.* - John MacArthur, The Danger of False Teaching (sermon), http://tinyurl.com/j5f36wb

It has got to be obvious that I think Sarah Young's devotional book *"Jesus Always"* is poisonous false teaching that must be avoided. But, I going further than that, I'm telling you to proactively run from it.

Why Run?

Why do I continually tell you to RUN from *"Jesus Always?"* Why don't I just say, "Don't read it?" There is an important difference.

Running is the Biblical response. It means to actively avoid the *"Jesus Always"* devotional. Not reading something is passive, and as a result there is a possibility others may be harmed.

For example, let's say someone gives you a copy of *"Jesus Always"* as a gift. You never open it. You just put it on your bookshelf. Some friends come visiting, and one of them notices *"Jesus Always."* They don't say anything, but they assume that since you are a good Christian, and you have a copy of *"Jesus Always,"* it must be a good devotional. So they buy a copy for themselves and make it their daily devotional. You are responsible for harming that person.

Running from *"Jesus Always"* means to be proactive. It means taking action to ensure neither you, nor your family, nor anyone else is harmed. That means do not ever have a copy in your home. Run from it! If someone gives you a copy, throw it away.

Where Does Scripture Say To Run From False Teaching?

John wrote a letter to "the chosen lady and her children" urging her to totally avoid false teachers:

> *If anyone comes to you and does not bring this teaching, do not receive him into your house, and do not give him a greeting; for the one who gives him a greeting participates in his evil deeds.* - 2 John 10 & 11

An article on the Got Questions web site explains what John is saying:

> *"It is important to understand the context of John's epistle. John is writing to "the elect lady and her children" (verse 1). This lady was engaged in a ministry of hospitality. In the name of Christian love (verse 6), this kind-hearted woman was receiving itinerant preachers into her home, providing room and board for them, and sending them on their way with her blessing.*

John writes this quick note to her to warn her about the many false teachers who would gladly take advantage of her generosity. Her love needed to be tempered by truth. Boundaries had to be drawn. Hospitality should not be extended to charlatans, hucksters, and the devil's own emissaries." - http://www.gotquestions.org/allow-false-teachers-home.html

Then the Apostle John takes it even further, not only should she not allow them in her home, she should not even greet them -- *for the one who gives him a greeting participates in his evil deeds.*

What is the principle John is teaching? Don't do anything that helps false teachers. This includes doing things that might cause others to believe you support or endorse their teaching. If you greet a false teacher, someone seeing you do this might think you are in fellowship with the false teacher and supportive of what they teach.

Yes, false teaching is that serious of a problem. You cannot take the chance that someone will mistakenly think you support the false teaching.

Did the Apostle John Practice What He Preached?

Cerinthus, one of the early leaders of the Gnostic movement (a false teaching very similar to New Age) lived at the same time as the Apostle John. A story is told about a time when John and some of his disciples were going to a bathhouse. As he was entering John learned that Cerinthus was inside. John turned, and ran from the building shouting, *"Let us flee, lest the building fall down; for Cerinthus, the enemy of the truth, is inside!"*

John physically ran from the false teacher Cerinthus, not because he feared Cerinthus, but to protect the truth. If John was seen in fellowship with Cerinthus, that would have, for some people, put John's stamp of approval on the heresy of Gnosticism.

That is why we need to run from books we know are presenting false teaching such as *Jesus Always*. Biblical truth is precious and brings life to the lost. We must be willing to sacrifice ourselves to protect the truth. We must be proactive in running from false teaching (including lectures, videos, books, magazines, music, sermons, etc.) so that we never, even inadvertently, do anything that might give the appearance we approve of the false teaching.

False Teachers – Isn't The Problem Obvious?

- False teachers, and false teaching such as *Jesus Always*, can be difficult to spot because they disguise themselves as teachers of righteousness… as the source of new truth and insights… as the source of spiritual light. That's exactly what *Jesus Always* does:

For such men are false apostles, deceitful workers, disguising themselves as apostles of Christ. No wonder, for even Satan disguises himself as an angel of light. - 2 Corinthians 11:13-14

- False teachers are difficult to spot because their false teaching is almost always mixed with truth. The prosperity preachers on TV talk about the importance of scripture. They will call on the name of Jesus. They will describe the multitude of missionaries they support and the on-going good work they do. They pray. They quote Jesus. They sound very spiritual and religious… but it's all just to get you to pull out your credit card and send them money.

- False teachers often appear to be nicer, more spiritual, and more loving than true preachers of the gospel. They usually have great smiles, a friendly attitude, wonderful personalities, and they dress well. But, they are like the Pharisees, it is all external. It is nothing more than the sugar coating on a poison pill. Writing to Timothy about false teachers, Paul described them as,

"holding to a form of godliness, although they have denied its power; Avoid such men as these." – 2 Timothy 3:5

- False teaching, such as the teaching in *Jesus Always*, is particularly difficult to spot. It is hidden by Biblical sounding language and references to scripture, and mixed with some devotions that do contain some Biblical truth. This mixture of truth and falsehood serves to hide the false teaching, and deceive the reader into thinking they are getting good teaching.

Warren Smith quotes a well-known Christian figure as saying, *"To survive in the post modern church you need to speak out of both sides of your mouth."* (http://tinyurl.com/hvupmdh) And that is exactly what New Age practitioners and teachers do. They'll say one thing, and also say the opposite, proclaiming both as truth.

That's why we must always run from books with false teaching, least we lead someone else to fall into the trap, or even we ourselves are deceived. Even with our guard up we can fall into the trap of believing the false teaching. We must always be focused on the truth and glorifying God, and rejecting all that is false.

> *For false Christs and false prophets will arise and will show great signs and wonders, so as to mislead, if possible, even the elect.* – Matthew 24:24

Not only are we to run from false teaching ourselves we are to help others escape false teaching. Jude writes:

> *And have mercy on some, who are doubting; save others, snatching them out of the fire; and on some have mercy with fear, hating even the garment polluted by the flesh.* - Jude 22 & 23

Commenting on these verses in Jude, John MacArthur points out that they tell us to come to the aid of a Christian trapped in false teaching. He says that false teaching is:

> *...like a prairie fire with its malignancy. That's why in Jude 23 it says when you get near anybody in a false system, snatch them like a brand from the burning and watch out that you don't get your garment spotted by that stuff. It's a malignancy, it eats up the neighboring tissue and spreads its corrupting doctrine to infect other people rapidly. It runs rampant.* - John MacArthur sermon The Danger Of False Teaching, http://tinyurl.com/j5f36wb

False teachers, such as *Jesus Always*, seem to be nice, loving, and very spiritual, and their messages are not offensive... they are messages filled with "peace" and "love," but they point to the broad way that leads to destruction. Run from them!

> *Therefore, having these promises, beloved, let us cleanse ourselves from all defilement of flesh and spirit, perfecting holiness in the fear of God.* - 2 Corinthians 1:1

We need to walk, think, act, and live according to scripture, following the examples given in scripture. Don't follow false teaching (*Jesus Always*) masquerading as light.

> *Brethren, join in following my example, and observe those who walk according to the pattern you have in us. For many walk, of whom I often told you, and now tell you even weeping, that they are enemies of the cross of Christ, whose end is destruction, whose god is their appetite, and whose glory is in their shame, who set their minds on earthly things.* - Philippians 3:17-19

Scripture continually warns us to be on our guard and not be deceived:

> *See to it that no one takes you captive by philosophy and empty deceit, according to the tradition of men, according to the elementary principles of the world, rather than according to Christ.* - Colossians 2:8

Why Run From False Teaching?

Even true believers can be deceived, for a time, by false teaching. While you cannot lose your salvation, you can lose some of your rewards:

> *Watch yourselves, that you do not lose what we have accomplished, but that you may receive a full reward.* - 2 John 8

Scripture also warns us that, if we pay attention to false teaching, we may pass on that false teaching to others. In particular, if you are a pastor or teacher, scripture tells you that one of your responsibilities is to instruct the men in your church so that they do not teach what is empty or false.

WHY RUN FROM *JESUS ALWAYS*?

As I urged you upon my departure for Macedonia, remain on at Ephesus so that you may instruct certain men not to teach strange doctrines, nor to pay attention to myths and endless genealogies, which give rise to mere speculation rather than furthering the administration of God which is by faith. - 1 Timothy 1:3-4

Pastors, you have a special responsibility to protect your flock. This includes protecting them from false teaching. Too many times I've heard about pastors giving out copies of *Jesus Calling* without having read it.

The same thing will probably happen with this new devotional from Sarah Young. Please, know what you are giving to your people, and protect them from books such as *Jesus Calling* and *Jesus Always*.

> *Today's church cannot remain faithful if it tolerates false teachers and leaves their teachings uncorrected and unconfronted.* – Albert Mohler, False Prophets, False Teachers and Real Trouble, June 1, 2011, http://tinyurl.com/3rq2uf7

SHOULD YOU RUN FROM *JESUS ALWAYS*?

CHAPTER 4
WHY DOESN'T JESUS UNDERSTAND
WHAT HE SAID IN SCRIPTURE?
MATTHEW 24:4-25:30

If *Jesus Always* had been written in a way, other than having Jesus speaking, it would just be a one of many unbiblical and misleading devotional books. I wouldn't be writing this book. But, *Jesus Always* presents its false teaching as though Jesus is doing the teaching, and that is a major attack on the character and glory of God that cannot be ignored.

Jesus Regularly Quotes Scripture in *Jesus Always*

In the introduction to *Jesus Always* Sarah Young explains why she has included scripture within the devotions:

Because I revere the Bible, I always endeavor to make my writing consistent with Biblical truth. I include Scripture in the devotions (indicated with italics), and each entry is followed by three or four Bible references. I encourage you to look up and read these scriptures carefully, they are words of Life! – Sarah Young, *Jesus Always* Introduction, page xii

Let's be sure we understand what she is saying: Scripture is important, and because of that she has included scripture in the devotions. And because scripture is important, she has put it in italics so you'll know when you are reading scripture within a devotion. No other reason is given for words being italicized.

Okay, let's look at an example to see how well "Jesus" understands scripture. I flipped through *Jesus Always* and picked the June 10th devotion because I'm currently preaching a sermon series on the Olivet Discourse and this devotion references a parable Jesus tells in Olivet Discourse.

I typically put quotations in italics, but when quoting *Jesus Always* I will reproduce it exactly as it is printed in the book. That way you can see where Sarah Young uses italics, as well as how she uses punctuation and capitalization.

> "I am sovereign over the circumstances of your life, so there are always opportunities to be found in them. Don't be like the man who *hid his master's talent in the ground* because he was disgruntled with his circumstances. He gave up and took the easy way out, blaming his hard situation rather than making the most of his opportunity. Actually the more difficult your circumstances, the more you gain through it." - *Jesus Always*, June 10

The phrase "*hid his master's talent in the ground*" is in italics, identifying it as a quote (paraphrase) from scripture, Matthew 25:25:

> *And I was afraid, and went away and went and hid your talent in the ground."* – Matthew 25:25 (NKJV)

What Is This Parable Teaching?

The "Jesus" of *Jesus Always* says this parable is about a slave who is having a hard time. He has a tough master and he doesn't like his circumstances. He then does the wrong thing by giving up instead of making the most of an opportunity. According to *Jesus Always*, the point of the parable is that we need to make the most of every opportunity. The more difficult your circumstances, the more you can gain through properly responding to those tough circumstances. It sounds like good teaching, but is that what Jesus is really teaching? Nope. Not even close.

WHY DOESN'T JESUS UNDERSTAND SCRIPTURE?

The context is given in Matthew 24:31. Jesus has been describing the signs that will be seen prior to his return at the end of the Tribulation, and then he tells His disciples to be ready because:

He will send forth His angels with A GREAT TRUMPET and THEY WILL GATHER TOGETHER His elect from the four winds, from one end of the sky to the other. – Matthew 24:31

What are they to be ready for? The gathering together of His elect... the gathering together of those people who are saved. What do you need to do in order to be ready? You need to have repented and trusted in Jesus as your Savior. You need to be saved.

Jesus then tells four parables that illustrate what he is teaching (Matthew 24:4-31). The first two are:

1. The parable of the fig tree illustrates that there will be signs indicating His return is near. (Matthew 24:32-35)

2. The parable of the faithful and evil slaves shows that we are to be alert, even if it has been a long time and Jesus has not yet returned. (Matthew 24:42-51)

In the final two parables we see illustrations showing that true believers will be ready for the return of Christ, and false Christians will not. Their readiness will be seen in how they wait and what they do while they wait.

The third parable (Matthew 25:1-12) describes ten bridesmaids. There are five who have oil for their lamps. These are the ones who have spiritual life. They have repented and trusted Jesus as their Savior. They were not just waiting for the return of Jesus, they are ready for Him to return. They have their lamps as well as oil for their lamps.

The other five bridesmaids are also waiting for the bridegroom, signifying that they think they are saved. But, they are not ready because they do not have oil for their lamps.

The oil represents spiritual life. Although they think they are saved and they were part of the bridal party waiting for Jesus to come, they have not actually put their trust in Jesus as their Savior. They have no spiritual life (lamp oil) Thus, when He comes, the bridegroom (Jesus) says to them:

"Truly I say to you, I do not know you." -- Matthew 25:12

When the Lord appears at the end of the Tribulation, many professed Christians will frantically realize their lack of spiritual life. They will not have heeded Paul's advice to the Corinthian church: "Test yourself to see if you are in the faith; examine yourselves! Or do you not recognize this about yourselves, that Jesus Christ is in you—unless indeed you fail the test?" (2 Corinthians 13:5). They will be self-deceived, perhaps believing that mere association with the things and the people of Christ has made them a part of Christ's true church. Some may think that being born into a Christian family will make them a member of God's family. We know with certainty that many will be trusting in their good works. - John MacArthur, New Testament Commentary Matthew 24-28, 1989, page 90

All of this gives us the context for the fourth parable, the parable of the talents. This is the parable *Jesus Always* quotes. It illustrates that true believers will use the gifts God has given them to further God's kingdom. Here is what Jesus says in scripture:

For it is just like a man about to go on a journey, who called his own slaves and entrusted his possessions to them. To one he gave five talents, to another, two, and to another, one, each according to his own ability; and he went on his journey. Immediately the one who had received the five talents went and traded with them, and gained five more talents. In the same manner the one who had received the two talents gained two more. But he who received the one talent went away, and dug a hole in the ground and hid his master's money. – Matthew 25:14-18

Three trusted slaves are given money to manage while their master is away. The first two slaves manage the money such that it is doubled by the time their master returns. The third slave does nothing with what he is given. Instead he buries the money in the ground. He could have at least put it in the bank and collected interest, but he does nothing with what he was given.

The point of this parable, keeping it in its context, is that, how we use what God has given us is an indication of whether we are saved or not. Those who use their abilities to further God's kingdom, are doing God's will and this shows they are saved. Those who do not use their gifts at all, or use them in ways that oppose the kingdom, demonstrate by their action (or lack of action) that they are not saved and their eternal destiny is outer darkness (hell).

Jesus is using these parables to illustrate the difference between His true followers, and those who believe they are following Christ, but they are not truly followers of Christ. The third "slave" thought he was a slave of Christ and a kingdom resident. But, his actions proved him wrong. So Jesus says:

Throw out the worthless slave into the outer darkness; in that place there will be weeping and gnashing of teeth. – Matthew 25:30

How Does This Compare With *Jesus Always*?

In *Jesus Always* this important parable about the second coming and salvation is twisted to be a parable about dealing with difficult circumstances. The salvation message is totally gone. The "Jesus" of *Jesus Always* does not understand his own words in scripture! Not only that, as we'll see next, he attacks the character of God!

John MacArthur provides more details on what Jesus is teaching:

The third slave, however, did not present the master with earnings but with an accusatory and self-serving excuse. ...Like the other two, that slave was identified as belonging to the master (see v 14), representative of his belonging to Christ's church before the second coming. But in two distinct ways he proved that his identification with Christ was superficial and did not involve genuine faith or regeneration.

First of all, he produced absolutely nothing with the talent he had been given and did not even make an attempt to use it for his master's benefit and profit.

Second, this slave demonstrated his counterfeit allegiance by deprecating his master's character, accusing him of being "a hard man, reaping where he did not sow, and gathering where he had scattered no seed. He charged his owner with being unmerciful and dishonest. That slave represents the professing Christian whose limited knowledge of God leads him to conclude that He is distant, uncaring, unjust, and undependable. – John MacArthur, New Testament Commentary Matthew 24-28, 1989, page 105

In this parable the "master" represents God. Based on the *Jesus Always* interpretation, what type of character does God have? He is unmerciful and dishonest. According to *Jesus Always* the third slave could have been the hero of the story, if only he realized he needed to persevere and overcome the difficult circumstances resulting from his master's (God's) harsh character. That's wrong! That's defaming God's character and degrading God's glory. The slave is judging and condemning the character of God! This is unbelievable for a supposedly "Christian" devotional book!

Why doesn't the "Jesus" of *Jesus Always* understand his own parable? Why does the "Jesus" of *Jesus Always* slander God's character instead of glorifying God?

BECAUSE HE IS NOT THE REAL JESUS. YOU CANNOT TRUST THE JESUS OF *JESUS ALWAYS."* This is not a Christian devotional book. You cannot trust *Jesus Always* to give you scriptural truth.

RUN FROM *JESUS ALWAYS!*

I wish I could end this chapter here, but I can't. We were looking at the phrases in italics in the June 10th devotion and there is more that needs to be said. Remember, these phrases are in italics to identify them as coming from scripture. Here is the last paragraph:

"I gladly give you Glory-strength. It is exceedingly potent because the Spirit Himself empowers you-- *strengthening you in your inner being.* Moreover, My limitless Glory-strength enables you to keep on *enduring the unendurable.* Since this Power is so vast, there is more than enough of it to *spill over into Joy!*" – *Jesus Always*, June 10

First, what is "Glory-strength?" That's not a Biblical term. I'd like to keep the focus on scripture, so I'll only take a moment to talk about this word. It refers to god who is in and is a part of Glory (capital "G"), and you having the ability to draw on this glory-source of energy, power, and strength (like the force in Star Wars.) The phrase "Glory-strength" means nothing to a Christian, but it is a significant phrase for followers of New Age teaching. Watch for these capitalized hyphenated words throughout *Jesus Always*. They indicate New Age teaching. Now, back to scripture…

Notice that several phrases in this quote are in italics. It is interesting that, if you do a Google search for the second phrase, what Google finds is that *"enduring the unendurable"* is a quote from Emperor Hirohito's speech given on August 15, 1945 when Japan surrendered and World War II ended. But, nothing Biblical shows up.

But wait! What about the Bible translation known as *The Message*? It says:

> *We pray that you'll have the strength to stick it out over the long haul—not the grim strength of gritting your teeth but the glory-strength God gives. It is strength that endures the unendurable and spills over into joy, thanking the Father who makes us strong enough to take part in everything bright and beautiful that he has for us.* – The Message, the last two sentences of Colossians 1:9-12

There it is. "Jesus" is paraphrasing *The Message*. That's amazing! *The Message* is a paraphrase. So "Jesus" is paraphrasing a paraphrase. This is not good. But what's worse is that *The Message* is a bible "translation" with a lot of problems…. it's not a translation we can trust.

> *I purchased a copy and began to read and study this paraphrase more in depth. What I discovered stunned me. The Message is not only a poor paraphrase, but it is, in fact, heretical.* – Justin Peters, A Brief Summary of Passages Contained Within "The Message,"

http:www. justinpeters.org/images/TheMessage2.pdf

Are you familiar with the Lord's Prayer? Here is how *The Message* translates the Lord's Prayer.

> Our Father in heaven,
> Reveal who you are.
> Set the world right;
> Do what's best—
>   as above, so below.
> Keep us alive with three square meals.
> Keep us forgiven with you and forgiving others.
> Keep us safe from ourselves and the Devil.
> You're in charge!
> You can do anything you want!
> You're ablaze in beauty!
>   Yes. **Yes.** Yes. – *The Message*

There are A LOT of things wrong with this. But let's make note of just one line… the words *"as above, so below."* This is a New Age saying meaning that we are all one, because god is within everyone. That's not Biblical.

> *One of the many examples of the New Age implications of* The Message *["Bible"] is seen in Eugene Peterson's paraphrasing of the Lord's Prayer. Where most translations read "on [or in] earth, as it is in heaven," Peterson inserts the occult/New Age phrase "as above, so below." The significance of this mystical occult saying is seen clearly in* As Above, So Below, *a book published in 1992 by the editors of* New Age Journal. *Chief editor Ronald S. Miller describes how the occult/magical saying "as above, so below" conveys the "fundamental truth about the universe"—the teaching that "we are all one" because God is "immanent" or "within" everyone and everything.* – Warren Smith, The New Age Implications of The Message "Bible" As Above, So Below, https://www.lighthousetrailsresearch.com/blog/?p=10403

What we have is a New Age devotional (*Jesus Always*) quoting a

New Age "translation of the Bible (*The Message*) to support the New Age teaching in the devotional. Avoid this devotional! RUN from Sarah Young and the *Jesus Always* devotional!

SHOULD YOU RUN FROM *JESUS ALWAYS*?

CHAPTER 5
SPOTTING NEW AGE TEACHING

Before going deeper into *Jesus Always* we should take a few moments to learn some of the characteristics of the New Age teaching commonly seen in *Jesus Always*. Not only will this help you spot the false teaching in *Jesus Always*, it will also help you identify New Age teaching in other books, videos, TV shows, and sermons.

What Is New Age?

In his book *"A Time Of Departing,"* Ray Yungen defines New Age as:

> *The Age of Aquarius, supposedly the Golden Age, when man becomes aware of his power and divinity.* – Ray Yungen, A Time of Departing, 2006, page 204

This sounds like a fad from the 60's that has come and gone. But don't be deceived. New Age spirituality is bigger than ever, and it is everywhere. Later in his book Ray Yungen writes:

> *Christian Yoga, spiritual disciplines, spiritual formation, the silence, sacred space, and contemplative prayer—do any of these sound familiar? If you haven't heard of them yet, chances are it's just a matter of time before these terms start showing up in your church.* – Ray Yungen, A Time of Departing, 2006, page 204

Author and speaker Warren Smith was deeply immersed in the New Age Movement. At the height of his involvement with New Age:

"the Lord intervened. He exposed the darkness that was actually behind the deceptive "peace," "love," and "light" of our New Age/New Gospel teachings. By the time it was all over, it was clear to us that all of our New Age beliefs had been founded on half-truths and lies." Warren Smith, blog post, http://tinyurl.com/gr78lpj

In his book *"False Christ Coming, Does Anybody Care?"* Warren describes the "Jesus" of the New Age Movement[1]:

The New Age Gospel teaches that when humanity collectively accepts and experiences itself as being part of Christ and a part of God, we will not only save ourselves, we will save our world... With "new revelation" often accompanied by direct personal spiritual experience, people are taught that because they are a part of God, they are actually "at-one" with God and all creation. – Warren Smith, False Christ Coming, Does Anybody Care?, 2011, Pages 13 & 14

New Age teaching and practices are growing in our churches, and it is moving into our schools. I regularly receive flyers from organizations that train teachers in how to use New Age techniques. They don't mention the phrase "New Age," but they offer training in New Age practices such as *"Yoga & Mindfulness for Kids"* (from an organization known as PESI), and *"Calming The Overactive Brain"* (offered by the Institute For Brain Potential).

So what does this have to do with *Jesus Always*? I've reproduced the front of a mailer from PESI on the next page. Be aware that the word "Yoga" is the Sanskirt word meaning unity. Yoga is a Sanatan Dharma practice that is a foundational part of Hinduism (New Age). It is the way to achieve unity with the Hindu Gods. Notice how Yoga is described in this flyer as being: *"a wonderful introduction to present-moment awareness and mindfulness."*

---

1 - I recommend Warren Smith's books for those who are interested in learning more about New Age/New Gospel beliefs. Visit: www.WarrenBSmith.com

"Little Flower Yoga for Kids is a wonderful introduction to present-moment awareness and mindfulness through a grounded and playful yoga practice. It is an inspiring resource for children and their parents."

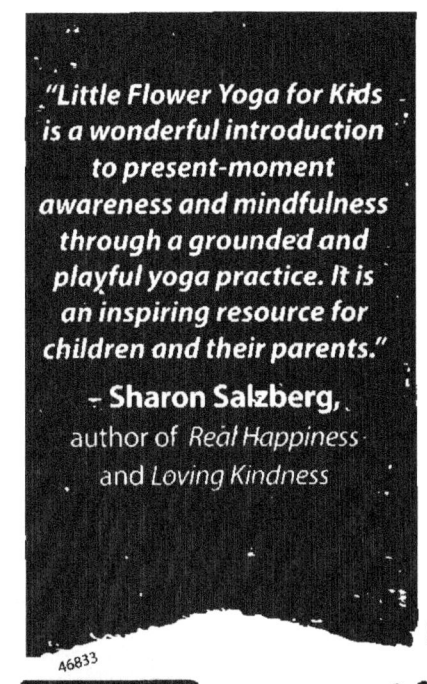

— Sharon Salzberg, author of *Real Happiness* and *Loving Kindness*

Yoga & Mindfulness for Kids: Improve Emotional Regulation and Increase Attention

This describes some of the New Age practices we see in *Jesus Always*, none of which are Biblical. The most common New Age practices you'll be taught to use by *Jesus Always* include:

Present-moment awareness: this means to not think about the past, nor worry about the future, but to focus on the present. It is a technique for emptying the mind so you can come into the presence of "god."

Mindfulness: is similar to present-moment awareness. It involves focusing on being calm in the present moment, and accepting your feelings and whatever you are experiencing. It is another technique for emptying the mind so you can come into the presence of "god."

"Mindfulness means paying attention in a particular way; on purpose, in the present moment, and nonjudgmentally." - Jon Kabat-Zinn, founder of the Mindfulness-Based Stress Reduction program at the University of Massachusetts Medical Center

Oneness with God: this is commonly taught in *Jesus* Always through what is called Practicing the Presence (of god). Practicing the Presence, or sometimes it is just referred to as the Presence (with a capital "P") involves sitting quietly, often whispering a simple word or phrase to help you empty your mind and experience the presence of god. As you calm and silence your mind, the god who is within you (oneness with god) may be experienced.

Capitalized Words: because New Age theology teaches that god is everything and everything is god, you'll see many words capitalized that typically are not capitalized. For example, words such as Peace, Joy, Love, and Refuge This sure sign of New Age teaching is the result of the belief that these are a direct reference to god.

The Silence: this refers to emptying your mind of all thoughts; *"to suspend thought through word repetition or breath focus—inward mental silence. Tilden Edwards called this the 'bridge to far Eastern spirituality.'"*[2]

---

2   Ray Yungen, A Time of Departing, 2009, page 88

Repetition/Breath Focus: these are two of the most common practices used to help empty your mind.

Repetition refers to repeating a single word or phrase. This might be the name of "Jesus," a phrase such as "I love you Jesus," or some scripture. Throughout *Jesus Always* you will encounter exhortations to pray short prayers such as these.

Breath focus means you are to slow and control your breathing, often by saying one word or phrase as you inhale, and another as you exhale.

Look for these practices, or variations of them, in *Jesus Always*. You'll find them throughout the book. **None of these are Biblical.** None of these are in scripture. We never see Jesus, nor any of the apostles… nor anyone in scripture using any of these practices. You should follow their example. Do not use any of the New Age practices taught by the *Jesus Always* devotional.

Do they work? Yes, but not in the way they promise. You can do these things and feel very spiritual, and feel very close to god. You can do these things and feel good… calm and relaxed. But they are not Biblical and they are bringing you spiritually closer to something that is not of God.

Remember what scripture says, the true battle is not happening in a realm you can see:

> *For our struggle is not against flesh and blood, but against the rulers, against the powers, against the world forces of this darkness, against the spiritual forces of wickedness in the heavenly places.* – Ephesians 6:12

You are in a battle against spiritual forces of darkness, and they will do whatever it takes to draw you away from the true Jesus Christ… such as making you feel good when using practices that open you to demonic influence. For example, by successfully getting you to sin (doing things God does not want you to do, such as the New Age practices in *Jesus Always*), demons have the ability to influence you and your feelings. They can make you feel good, and give you calm, peaceful feelings that make you feel very spiritual and close to "god." Why would a demon want to help you to feel good? To lead you away from the true Jesus Christ, the Son of God, the only one who can save you. Using the New Age practices described in this chapter opens you to these demonic spiritual forces.

SHOULD YOU RUN FROM *JESUS ALWAYS*?

The result of the battle may depend on whether you are truly saved. False Christians have few defenses against demonic oppression. They have the common grace that is available to all, but they do not have the Holy Spirit indwelling them. And without the Holy Spirit they cannot resist the devil.

For the true Christian, victory over demonic oppression is always available through the power of the indwelling Holy Spirit, if we do as Peter says in 1 Peter 5:9 and resist the devil. To resist the devil means relying on the Holy Spirit, not our own power, to successfully resist demonic influence.

But for both the true believer and the false believer, if you practice what *Jesus Always* teaches, you open yourself to demonic oppression. For example, do you remember what scripture says happened to the man who was cleaned out and left empty? He was in the condition New Age practices strive to achieve... he was ready for demons to move in.

> *Now when the unclean spirit goes out of a man, it passes through waterless places seeking rest, and does not find it. Then it says, "I will return to my house from which I came"; and when it comes, it finds it unoccupied, swept, and put in order. Then it goes and takes along with it seven other spirits more wicked than itself, and they go in and live there; and the last state of that man becomes worse than the first.*—Matthew 12:43-45

What should he have done after the unclean spirit left? Put on the new man (Colossians 3:10). Put on the things of God... put on the character of God. You were created in the image of God. Be who you were created to be. God has given you a new heart and a new life... put on that new life.

What should you do when you encounter someone teaching the practices in this chapter? What should you do when you encounter a book or DVD promoting these practices? RUN! New Age practices are similar to the occult, and are very dangerous. Don't get anywhere near them. Don't let them into your life. Tightly shut and lock the door to your mind and feelings. Fill your thoughts with scripture, fill your life with the character of God. Turn to and trust the true Jesus in scripture.

CHAPTER 6
WHY DOESN'T JESUS UNDERSTAND PSALM 46?

Let's look at another *Jesus Always* devotion. I'd like to keep it simple and just turn the page in *Jesus Always* to look at the devotion for June 11th. Here is the last paragraph:

> Since My methods of working in the world are often mysterious, it's important to take time to *be still and know that I am God*. Sit quietly in My Presence, breathing My Peace, and I will give you rest. – *Jesus Always*, June 11th

Wow! From what we just learned about New Age, "Jesus" says a lot of dangerous things in just this one sentence. It is packed with encouragement to participate in unbiblical New Age practices. Notice the following (referring back to the previous chapter):

- The focus on being still (sit quietly.)
- Breath focus ("breathing My Presence")
- "Peace" is capitalized.
- My Presence (being in the Presence, with a capital "P")
-

Let's begin by focusing on scripture. "Jesus" quotes Psalm 46, verse 10, from the NIV: This is a verse commonly used by New Age teachers to support the practice of silencing your mind.

He says, "Be still, and know that I am God; - Psalm 46:10a

SHOULD YOU RUN FROM *JESUS ALWAYS?*

What is *Jesus Always* saying here? Going back to be beginning of the June 11th devotion, it appears it is about sitting quietly and resting in Jesus. Here are the first two sentences:

> **MY PRESENCE WILL GO WITH YOU, and I will give you rest. Wherever you are, wherever you go, I am with you!** – *Jesus Always*, June 11th

The first sentence is in italic indicating it is also a quote from scripture. You'll find it is from Exodus 33:14 quoted from the NIV. We'll need to look at this verse, but let's start with Psalm 46.

The June 11th devotion opens by offering rest, and it closes by offering rest. Obviously the overall subject of the devotion is having rest.

"Jesus," in the final paragraph (quoted above), tells us to take the time to be still. "Jesus" further tells us to sit quietly and breathe in his Peace, and the result will be that he will give us rest.

It seems clear. "Jesus" is teaching us that, during our busy, stress-filled days, when we need rest, we need to be still, know Jesus is God, and sit quietly in his Presence. Is that what Psalm 46:10 is about?

Let's start with how New Age teachers understand this verse: It is a verse that is commonly used to promote the practice is sitting in silence so you can hear God's voice.

> *Eileen Caddy's New Age understanding of the "God within" and "oneness" started with an inner voice that told her "Be still and know that I am God." Like Caddy, so many people who have been raised in today's church have been similarly deceived into believing that the "be still" verse from Psalm 46:10 is God's heavenly instruction to enter into solitude and silence so they can hear His voice.* – Warren Smith, "Be Still and Know That YOU Are God? Is That Really What Scripture Says? blog post: http://tinyurl.com/heyedbl

It would be nice if we knew Sarah Young's thoughts about this verse... and we can. She explains her understanding of Psalm 46:10 in the introduction to her *Jesus Calling* book where she writes:

A life-changing verse has been "Be still and know that I am God." (Psalm 46:10). Alternate readings for "Be still" are "Relax," "Let go," and "Cease striving" (NASB). This is an enticing invitation from God to lay down our cares and seek His Presence. I believe that God yearns for these quiet moments with us even more than we do. I also believe that He still speaks to those who listen to Him (John 10:27), and I continually depend on the Holy Spirit's help in this. – Sarah Young, Introduction, *Jesus Calling*, 2004, page xiii.

This is consistent with what we read in the June 11th devotion in *Jesus Always*, as well as Warren Smith's description of the New Age understanding of this verse. We are to sit quietly… have quiet moments… and seek god's Presence within us. The only problem is, that's not what Psalm 46 is about.

What is God Actually Saying in Psalm 46?

This Psalm was the inspiration for Martin Luther's hymn, *"A Mighty Fortress Is Our God."* It is a Psalm about God's strength and trusting Him in faith and obedience. It is a Psalm of comfort, knowing that God is sovereign.

Few Psalms breathe the spirit of sturdy confidence in the Lord in the midst of very real danger as strongly as does this one. – H. C. Leupold, Exposition of the Psalms, 1959, page 363

Looking at the context, the first two verses of this Psalm establish the subject as our having comfort in times of distress:

*God is our refuge and strength,
a very present help in trouble.
Therefore we will not fear, though the earth should change
And though the mountains slip into the heart of the sea;*

The overall context is that of Israel facing danger. God is calling His people to have an attitude of faith and trust in Him. They are to place their confidence in God, and God will deliver them from the danger. That's why this Psalm inspired Luther to write *"A Mighty Fortress Is Our God."* This Psalm is not about sitting quietly waiting to feel God's presence. It's a Psalm about our God being a mighty fortress protecting us!

Charles Spurgeon quotes Jonathan Edwards in his commentary on Psalm 46:10, explaining what it means to be still:

> *Be still as to words; not speaking against the sovereign dispensations of providence, or complaining of them; not darkening counsel by words without knowledge, or justifying ourselves and speaking great swelling words of vanity. We must be still as to actions and outward behaviour, so as not to oppose God in his dispensations; and as to the inward frame of our hearts, cultivating a calm and quiet submission of soul to the sovereign pleasure of God, whatever it may be.* – Jonathan Edwards, (quoted by Charles Spurgeon), The Treasury of David, Psalm 46:10

"Be still" in Psalm 46:10 is not about resting. It does not mean to sit calmly and have some quiet time with Jesus as Sarah Young says. Immediately after quoting Edwards, Spurgeon also quotes Richard Cameron's July 18, 1680 sermon:

> *Be still, and know that I am God. This text of scripture forbids quarreling and murmuring against God.*

When facing mortal danger, we are to stop fighting against God. We are to stop complaining about God. We are to stop striving in our own wisdom and power, and TRUST God. "Be still" means we are to submit to God's will. We need to understand that He is sovereign, meaning whatever He wills, that is what will happen. God is in control, so we need to stop trying to take control away from Him... that is what "be still" means.

Psalm 46:10 -- Scripture vs. *Jesus Always*

Psalm 46:10 is about trusting the sovereignty of God. It is not about resting or silencing your thoughts. By the way, New Age teachers never quote the entire verse. Let's read all of it:

> *He says, "Be still, and know that I am God;*
> *I will be exalted among the nations,*
> *I will be exalted in the earth."* – Psalm 46:10

What is it that exalts God? Is it our sitting quietly, having a quiet moment with god, and waiting to hear his voice? Or is it our submitting to His will and trusting Him to save us from all danger? Which of these exalts and glorifies God? I'll take number two for ten points… and a win on this question.

Exodus 33:14

Now let's go back to the first scripture that was quoted, Exodus 33:14. Once again the phrase *"My Presence"* is used. Let's read the entire first paragraph:

> MY PRESENCE WILL GO WITH YOU, and I will give you rest. Wherever you are, wherever you go, I am with you! This is an astonishing statement, yet it is true. My unseen Presence is more *real* than the flesh-and-blood people around you. But you must "see" Me with the eyes of your heart and communicate with Me through prayer, trusting that I really do hear and care. – *Jesus Always*, June 11th

What does scripture say?

My Presence will go with you, and I will give you rest. – Exodus 33:14 (NIV)

Jesus Always has accurately quoted Exodus 33:14, and superficially it seems to agree with Sarah Young's interpretation. God is Present (capital "P in *Jesus Always*") with you now. He always will be with you, and he will give you rest.

What type of presence is Sarah Young talking about? It's a feeling that Jesus is present with you that results from sitting quietly and breathing "My Presence." When you do this, "Jesus" will give you rest. (See the quote at the beginning of the chapter.) Is this what Exodus 33 is talking about?

What Is Exodus 33:14 Actually Talking About?

To get the context we need to go back to Exodus 32:34. Led by Aaron the people had sinned by worshiping a golden calf while

Moses was on the mountain with God. In these verses Moses is pleading with God to forgive their sin, and the Lord replies to Moses:

> *"Whoever has sinned against Me, I will blot him out of My book. But go now, lead the people where I told you. Behold, My angel shall go before you."* - Exodus 32:33 & 34a

The key point is that, previously God had led them. But now they have seriously sinned, separating themselves from God. So God is no longer going to lead them. He says that He will send an angel to go before them. In the next chapter God again tells Moses He will send an angel to lead the people.

> *I will send an angel before you and I will drive out the Canaanite, the Amorite, the Hittite, the Perizzite, the Hivite and the Jebusite.* - Exodus 33:2

Before this God had been leading the Jews in the form of a pillar of cloud by day and a pillar of fire by night. Now God says that an angel will go before them. Moses sees that as a problem, and he wants to be sure God Himself continues to lead them.

> *And He said, "My presence shall go with you, and I will give you rest." Then he said to Him, "If Your presence does not go with us, do not lead us up from here. For how then can it be known that I have found favor in Your sight, I and Your people? Is it not by Your going with us, so that we, I and Your people, may be distinguished from all the other people who are upon the face of the earth?"* – Exodus 33:14-16

Moses is concerned that, if God's presence is not leading them, other nations and peoples will not know they have God's favor. God's presence, in a pillar of cloud by day and pillar of fire by night, is a powerful sign that God is with them.

What does the term *"My presence"* refer to in Exodus 33:14? A theophany. The presence of God in a form that can be seen by people. This is not a mystical, unseen presence as described in *Jesus Always*. This is a real presence in which God appears in a pillar of cloud and a pillar of fire.

The "Jesus" of *Jesus Always* has taken this verse out of context and given it a completely new meaning. Scripture is talking about a theophany. Sarah Young is talking about a mystical experience.

What does God mean when He says, *"I will give you rest"*? He is telling Moses He can trust God. God will continue to lead them as He has in the past. Moses, and all of the people, do not need to be concerned... there will continue to be a visible presence of God leading them through the wilderness. The message is very similar to Psalm 46:10: Moses, and all of Israel, can trust God's promise to be with them.

Once again the truth is very different from the meaning you get from reading the *Jesus Always* devotion. There is nothing in this devotion about "resting" because you can trust God's promises. And there is nothing in all of scripture telling you to sit quietly and wait until you become aware of God's presence. Scripture and *Jesus Always* are teaching two very different things.

Once again the "Jesus" of *Jesus Always* does not correctly understand scripture. Are you going to follow the teaching of the false New Age Jesus of *Jesus Always*, or are you going to trust scripture? I hope you choose the truth of scripture.

SHOULD YOU RUN FROM *JESUS ALWAYS*?

CHAPTER 7
BREAK TIME
(A DIFFERENT TAKE ON THE PROBLEM OF JESUS SPEAKING)

Let's take a short break from our analysis of *Jesus Always* and look at Sarah Young having Jesus speaking in *Jesus Always* from a different perspective.

So far it's looking like Sarah Young's "Jesus" does not know very much about scripture. That's a deal killer. I cannot follow a Jesus (or author) who does not teach a correct understanding of scripture. But, there are other problems.

Imagine you have some ideas about how to be a successful TV talk show host. You've watched a lot of talk shows over the past decades and you have a ton of notes and observations on what makes a good talk show. In particular you've focused on Oprah and what she did to become successful.

So you decide to write a book. You organize your notes, and compile a set of 365 short guidelines to help your readers become successful TV talk show hosts... and you write them as though Oprah was speaking them. It's just as though you were quoting Oprah, but you are supplying the words. What do you think will happen?

You'd get sued so quickly, and for such a huge amount of money, that your head would spin. And YOU WOULD LOSE the lawsuit. The court will side with Oprah. You've done wrong.

If you had written a book that actually quoted Oprah, such that everything was a real quote, there would have been no problem. But, you put words that Oprah didn't say, into her mouth. The result is that you may be paying off the court judgment for the rest of your life.

What I'm describing is exactly what Sarah Young has done. She's put words in Jesus' mouth that He never said. If we recognize this as a crime against Oprah, why don't we recognize what Sarah Young has done as a crime against God?

A Quick Test

Here is a quick test you can try. Just before reading a devotion from *Jesus Always*, say the following phrase out loud: *"This is not Jesus speaking."* Keep this phrase in your mind as you read the devotion... *this is not Jesus speaking.*

Does it bother you to say these words? Why? Remember, Sarah Young does not claim it is Jesus speaking. These devotions are her *"Personal reflections from her daily quiet time of Bible reading, praying, and writing in prayer journals."* (*Jesus Always*, About The Author, page 383)

In addition, as you've seen from the two devotions we've looked at so far, this "Jesus" does not understand scripture at all. There is no way the "Jesus" of *Jesus Always"* is anything more than a figment of Sarah Young's imagination. So when you are thinking *"this is not Jesus speaking"* as you read the devotion, you are thinking the truth. You have filled your mind with the truth.

If this test makes you feel uncomfortable, then you know there is a problem, and the problem is not with the knowledge that this is not Jesus speaking. The problem is with the book you are reading.

This is a simple test, and it is far from foolproof. But, from this simple exorcise I hope you will realize this is not Jesus speaking in *Jesus Always*. To put words He did not say in the mouth of Jesus is to make Jesus appear to be a liar.

> *...you will know the truth, and the truth will make you free.* - John 8:32

Don't ever forget. Jesus is not a person like you, HE IS GOD. Sarah Young is putting words on the lips of God that God never spoke[3].

---

3 -I recommend reading the *"Who's Calling?"* article in the Web Exclusive section of our web site: www.NotJesusCalling.com.

CHAPTER 8
"MY PRESENCE"
WHAT DOES THIS MEAN?

Error is not always obvious and so we need to be aware of the subtlety of error. This was clearly a problem in the early church. "For certain people have crept in unnoticed who long ago were designated for condemnation, ungodly people, who pervert the grace of our God into sensuality and deny our only Master and Lord, Jesus Christ" (Jude 4). – Tim Challies, The Discipline of Spiritual Discernment, 2007, page 103

Jesus Always regularly talks about "My Presence." What does this mean? There are some subtle shades of meaning we'll need to understand, so let's start by learning a little about discernment.

Deception can be hard to spot. For example, Satan disguises himself as an angel of light. He sends his demons to you as angels of light. They come proclaiming that they will show you the way to become closer to God. They proclaim they can show you how to feel calm and less anxious… how to feel happy… how to feel fulfilled… how to feel spiritual. And they can temporarily deliver on those promises of good feelings.

Satan, once the mightiest of the angels, is now the devil on the prowl for those who have forsaken him and who are seeking after God. Satan seeks to lead us astray. His tactics rarely change, for since the dawn of human history they have proven remarkably effective. Satan seeks to lead us astray, to deceive us, by offering us a counterfeit version of the truth. Satan offers something that resembles the truth but is actually error. He is craft and subtle, offering something that seems so close yet is still so far away. – Tim Challies, The Discipline of Spiritual Discernment, 2007, page 43

That's the problem. What Satan promises can sound very appealing and it may be close to the truth. But, what he promises are experiences an\t feelings, and what you need is a Savior. Satan's promises typically leave out one crucial component... the real Son of God and salvation through repentance and trusting in Jesus alone as your Savior. Oh, "Jesus" will be there, but it will be a counterfeit Jesus who cannot save you. That's what the "Jesus" of *Jesus Always* offers when he talks about "My Presence," "The Practice of Presence," or just "Presence" (with a capital "P")... it's all about an experience... your feelings... and that's all. There is no substance. No Jesus.

> **Do not be satisfied with only thinking about Me or knowing Me intellectually. Thirst for experiential knowledge of Me grounded in sound biblical truth.** - Sarah Young, Jesus Always, July 6

This statement is wrong in many ways. Nowhere does scripture tell us to seek feel-good experiences (experiential knowledge). The scriptural truth is that we are to hunger and thirst for righteousness (Jesus' words in Matthew 5:6). That's what we are to seek. We are to feed on God's Word so that we can grow in righteousness.

Practicing the Presence

One of the major themes in *Jesus Always* is that of the Presence of Jesus. The word "Presence" (with a capital "P") is used in many of the devotions. This is an important word and an important concept to understand. It is also a thoroughly New Age practice. So whenever *Jesus Always* starts talking about "Presence," warning lights should start flashing in your head.

What Does *Jesus Always* say about Presence? We've already seen some aspects of "Presence" in the June 11th devotion. So let's take a look at it again, plus what some of the other devotions say:

> ***My Presence will go with you, and I will give you rest...*** **It's important to take time to** *be still and know that I am God.* **Sit quietly in My**

"MY PRESENCE," WHAT DOES THIS MEAN?

Presence, breathing in My Peace, and I will give you rest. – June 11th

Come Rest with Me, beloved. Though many tasks are calling you, urging you to put them first, *I* know what you need most: to *be still* in My Presence. Take some deep breaths, and fix your gaze on Me…. Whisper My Name, "Jesus," in sweet remembrance of My nearness. – August 9th

When you relax in My Presence, trusting in My finished work on the cross, both you and I are refreshed. – August 24th

Okay, I picked one (August 24th) in which the cross is mentioned, so many of you are thinking, *"This is good. Jesus mentioned the cross. So this devotional book must be okay."*

Mentioning the cross, or using other Christian words, does not make a book Christian. Even talking about sin and Jesus' finished work on the cross does not make a book Christian. Try the test on the next page.

Defining "Presence"

Based on the above quotes do you understand what the phrase *"My Presence"* means? I don't. We can make some assumptions, but "Presence" is never defined. And what's with the "P" being capitalized?

The term "presence" may be defined in two ways. One is the New Age definition and the other is the Biblical definition… and they are very different. In this chapter we'll talk about the New Age definition and the way "Presence" is most often used in *Jesus Always*. Please note, there are a couple of devotions in *Jesus Always* that use the term "presence" somewhat biblically, but they are the few exceptions. And that's to be expected. It makes sorting truth from false more difficult.

Let's start with the question: Why is the word "Presence" capitalized? In fact, as I mentioned earlier, you may notice other words such as: Joy, Peace, Power, Glory, Glory-strength, Love-light, Strength, and Love are capitalized in *Jesus Always*. What's with all this extra capitalization? Douglas Groothuis explains:

Can You Identify False Teachers?
Is the following quote from a biblical teacher or a false teacher?

The Bible tells us very clearly that Christ is the only way to God and eternal life, and in Romans 10:9–11, the Bible tells us how to be saved and have eternal life: Believe in our hearts that Jesus died for our sins and was raised from the grave, and confess with our mouths that He is our Lord and Savior.

To be saved and to receive all that Jesus has done for you, you can make Him your Lord and Savior today by praying this prayer:

"Lord Jesus, thank You for loving me and dying for me on the cross. Your precious blood washes me clean of every sin. You are my Lord and my Savior, now and forever. I believe that You rose from the dead and that You are alive today. Because of Your finished work, I am now a beloved child of God and heaven is my home. Thank You for giving me eternal life, and filling my heart with Your peace and joy. Amen."
(http://tinyurl.com/j5v5fck)

What do you think? True or false teacher? It sounds very good, but false teachers can sound biblical. This is a quote from Joseph Prince, a prosperity gospel preacher. (http://tinyurl.com/jj7ghwt) He's a false teacher who twists scripture to support the claim that God guarantees health and wealth in this life. False teachers may talk about Jesus and salvation, they quote scripture, and they can sound very good while feeding people poisonous lies.

A common verse that is misused is Romans 10:9-10. To correctly understand this verse you need to know the historical context. In Paul's day to "confess with your mouth" was not just saying words. You were required to confess Caesar as lord. If you refused, the most likely result was death. To confess Jesus as Lord instead of Caesar was risking your life. What Paul is in effect saying is: you have a gun at your head. If you confess Jesus as Lord you'll be killed. In this circumstance, facing death, if you openly confess with your mouth (speak out loud so everyone hears you) Jesus as your Lord and Savior, you must truly be saved.

"MY PRESENCE," WHAT DOES THIS MEAN?

The great Oneness of Being is thought to be "God." All that is, at the metaphysical root, is God. [God is] some abstract entity, usually capitalized, like Infinite Intelligence, Principle, etc. We could add to this list "the Force," "Consciousness," "Energy" and so on. The New Age "God" is not a moral being worshiped as supreme. –Douglas Groothuis, Confronting the New Age, 1988, page 22

What Groothuis is saying is that the capitalized words are god. So when you say the word "Presence" you are directly referring to god. When you say the word "Peace," that is a direct reference to god. God is within us, and we are in him, and we are him. God is in everyone, and even within abstract concepts such as Joy, Peace and Love. These are not just attributes of god, they are indwelt by god.

"New age matriarch Alice Bailey, New Age leader Barbara Marx Hubbard, and countless other New Age/New Spirituality figures have used the term presence to refer to the "God" and "Christ" of the New Age movement. – Warren Smith, Another Jesus Calling, 2013, page 88.

As Swami Muktanada expressed it, God dwells within you as you. Or we may cite the story of the great American mystic Joel S. Goldsmith. One day he welcomed a woman into his office who was wanting to talk about God. "Oh, and what do you know about God?" Goldsmith asked. "Well," the woman said, "I know that I am part of God." "My dear madam," Goldsmith replied tenderly, "you are the whole of God." – Paul Weiss, Moonlight Leaning Against an Old Rail Fence, 2015, Commentary: Cosmology chapter.

Divinity is not outside us. We are in God and God in us. That is the unitive experience of the mystics East or West. – Matthew Fox, The Coming of the Cosmic Christ. Page 50

That's very different from the Christian view of God. By capitalizing these words, *Jesus Always* shows it has a different understanding of God than what the Holy Bible teaches. This is not a Christian book

In New Age theology god is in everything and everyone. You don't need to talk about god. Instead, because he is in everything, you just talk about the Presence.

This also means you don't need to go to an outside source, such as the Holy Bible, for knowledge of god. Because god is within you, you look within yourself to find god. That's why, for example, we need to enter the silence... meaning to empty our minds of our thoughts and worries, and minimize the self so the god within us can be felt and heard. We become aware of god by becoming quiet and stopping our own thoughts, worries, planning, and concerns[4].

Here is a quote from Sarah Young's first book describing what it feels like to come into the Presence:

> *One night I found myself leaving the warmth of our cozy chalet to walk alone in the snowy mountains. I went into a deeply wooded area, feeling vulnerable and awed by cold, moonlit beauty. The air was crisp and dry, piercing to inhale. Suddenly I felt as if a warm mist enveloped me. I became aware of a lovely Presence, and my involuntary response was to whisper, `Sweet Jesus.' This utterance was totally uncharacteristic of me, and I was shocked to hear myself speaking so tenderly to Jesus. As I pondered this brief communication, I realized it was the response of a converted heart; at that moment I knew I belonged to Him. This was far more than the intellectual answers for which I'd been searching. This was a relationship with the Creator of the universe.* – Sarah Young, Jesus Calling, 2004, page VII.

I noticed several things in the above quote:

- Coming into the Presence is a feeling... it is an experience.

- This is her testimony... with no mention of sin, repentance, commitment to Jesus as Lord, nor a changed life.

- This experience was *"far more than the intellectual answers for which I'd been searching."* This illustrates the fact that for New Agers feelings and experience are more important than knowledge. Yet over and over in Paul's prayers, He asks that God give believers "knowledge" of His will. (See Colossians 1:9, for

---

4 - If you need to silence your own thoughts so that you can hear god speak, this must be a very weak god. But, apparently the Jesus of *Jesus Always* cannot make himself known or heard unless you silence yourself. This "Jesus" is very weak and is not worthy of your worship.

example.) In scripture knowledge is important. In New Age knowledge takes a back seat to experiences and feelings.

How is the New Age experience of practicing the Presence accomplished? Here is what one expert says you need to do:

> *Living "in the now" has been a recurrent theme in my experiments. There is literally no way to practice God's presence if we are being pulled into the past (via shame, regret, etc.) or into the future (via worry). The only time in which we meet with God is the present moment, but very few people actually know how to live there.* – Scott Holman, Some Practical Tips on Practicing the Presence of God, http://tinyurl.com/h7ds226

Jesus in *Jesus* Always urges you to forget about the past; don't think about the future; be in the present only. Then you will experience god's Presence. It sounds just like New Age to me.

God in Us

I said that in New Age theology god is "in" everything. From scripture we know that God is everywhere. He is omnipresent. Isn't that the same thing? No, it is not.

New Age is a panentheistic religion. Here is how Ray Yungen defines it:

> *This position of the panentheist is challenging to understand. Your outer personality is not God, but God is still in you as your true identity. This explains why mystics say, "all is one." At the mystical level, they experience this God force that seems to flow through everything and everybody. All creation has God in it as a living, vital presence. It is just hidden.*

> *The theological implications of this worldview put it in direct odds with biblical Christianity for obvious reasons. Only one true God exists, and His identity is not in everyone. The fullness of God's identity, in bodily form, rests in Jesus Christ and Him only!* – Ray Yungen, A Time of Departing, 2006, pages 29 & 30

To summarize what Ray is saying, New Age theology states that god is all that exists. He is the entire universe, as well as transcending the universe. This means we all are a little part of god and god is part of us. That's who we truly are. And to be the person we truly are, we must reach the god within us… the Presence. This gives us access to god's power, strength, peace, etc. – the "force" within us[5].

That's New Age… that's the god of *Jesus Always*. But this is not the God of the Bible. Our true identity is not that of god. God is not a living Presence within everyone. God is not part of His creation (us), the true God exists outside of His creation. He is separate from His creation.

What about the Holy Spirit Dwelling In Us?

When you become a believer you have the Holy Spirit within you. This means you are no longer an enemy of God, and the Holy Spirit can now guide you, teach you, and illuminate scripture for you… and He is doing that from within you. But, He is not a part of you, nor are you a part of the Holy Spirit.

Christ also dwells in us, but, unlike New Age teaching, and this is the big difference: He is not a part of you and you are not a part of Him. In New Age thinking (e.g. *Jesus Always*) we are one with god and can reach and draw on the power of god within us. In scripture we learn the truth that we are united with Christ and the Holy Spirit indwells us, but they are not a part of us.

Yes, as Ray says, understanding New Age theology is challenging. Words are used in non-conventional ways, and it is vague in its definitions of itself. In addition, those definitions can change to adjust New Age beliefs to the specific situation. But I hope I've given you a basic understanding of the New Age concept of "Presence." I'll continue in the next chapter, as we look at the source of the idea of "Presence." Then we'll look at what the Bible means when talking about the presence of God.

---

5 - Think of this "force" as the force in Star Wars. It is everywhere, and in everything throughout the universe. By tapping into this force (the Presence) we have access to knowledge and power.

CHAPTER 9
THE TRUE PRESENCE OF JESUS

What do you mean, "A feeling of God's presence?" You could feel happy. You could feel sad. You could feel convicted of sin. You could have strong emotions over the joy that you felt; over the conviction that you felt; but one thing is for sure, you couldn't feel God's presence. God is a spirit. - John MacArthur, Is a feeling of God's Presence an Indication of True Worship? http://tinyurl.com/zcn2j36

Being in the Presence of God vs. the Presence of Jesus

To understand being in the presence of Jesus, we first must be sure we understand who Jesus is. He is God… the one and only creator God of the Bible. So when we talk about the "presence of God" and the "presence of Jesus" we are talking about the same thing. There is absolutely no difference in the meaning of these two phrases.

Being in Someone's Presence

When talking about other people, we say we are in the presence of someone when we are physically close to them. When we think about being in the presence of Jesus, we tend to impose this same definition… that Jesus is physically near. However, this not appropriate. We are close to God all the time, because God is everywhere. It is impossible to not be in the presence of God.

A second aspect of being in the presence of Jesus is that, when you become a Christian you are united with Christ (Romans 6:5, Galatians 2:20).

Or do you not recognize this about yourselves, that Jesus Christ is in you? – 2 Corinthians 13:5

In addition, as believers we also have the Holy Spirit (God) dwelling in us (1 Corinthians 3:16).

Guard, through the Holy Spirit who dwells in us, the treasure which has been entrusted to you. – 2 Timothy 1:14

So being physically in the presence of Jesus is not the issue. You can't get away from the presence of Jesus. God is omnipresent, meaning He is always present with everyone. And believers are united with Christ and have the Holy Spirit dwelling within them.

What Does It Mean Then, To Be In God's Presence?

Scripture talks about being in the presence of God in a number of different ways. These include:

- Being in God's presence in heaven.

- Being in the temple or tabernacle, where God's glory resides.

- Being physically with Jesus when He walked on the earth.

- Experiencing a theophany. A theophany is when God appears to someone, or a group of people, by taking on a physical appearance. Adam and Eve experienced the first theophany when they heard God walking in the garden. The Jews leaving Egypt where lead by a pillar of fire at night and a pillar of cloud during the day. These both are theophanies.

- Experiencing a dream or vision, or the reality of entering God's throne room. (Isaiah 6, Revelation 1)

Except for joining God in heaven when we die, these types of experiences do not happen in our present time. The temple does not exist; Jesus will not return until the end of the Tribulation time; and we have God's word in scripture, so theophanies, dreams, and visions are no longer needed. This leaves only one way in which we "experience" the presence of God in our daily lives. It is…

- We are always in the presence of God. We have knowledge of God's presence when we are notice that God is involved with the life of an individual, group, or a nation.

In these instances there is no visible manifestation of God's presence, but His presence is known through our recognizing His actions to either bless or pour out His wrath (curse). An example of this type of the "presence of God" is the Old Testament book of Esther. God is never mentioned in this book. No one ever prays. There is no worship nor crying out to God. There is nothing said about God. Yet, you can see the hand of God working, bringing about the preservation of the Jewish nation. The presence of G od is very evident.

(Recommended reading: *"The Presence of God, A Commentary on the Book of Esther"* by Steve Hudgik.)

In *Jesus Calling* Sarah Young describes God's presence as feeling like a warm mist. Others say it is a feeling of pure love… it feels like being enveloped in love. However, the one thing God's presence is not, is a feeling. We cannot feel God's presence and scripture never describes God's presence as a feeling.

God is always present, by the way, He's omnipresent. He doesn't come and He doesn't go. So you certainly couldn't feel His presence. You may have felt joy. You may have felt sorrow over sin. You may have felt guilt over your iniquity. You may have felt convicted. You could have felt those kinds of things in human emotion, as the word of God penetrates your heart, and you see glorious truth, you rejoice as it penetrates your heart, and you come up short, you feel sorrow. - John MacArthur Is a feeling of God's Presence an Indication of True Worship?
http://tinyurl.com/zcn2j36

Physically Coming into God's Presence

There are examples in scripture of people physically coming into God's presence. What happens? How do they feel? They are described as experiencing two things:

1 They immediately know God is good and they are not.

2. This results in feelings of fear, awe, total unworthiness, and the need to worship. People who experience God's presence in this way fall on their face. In Daniel's case, in Daniel 8:18 he fell on his face and passed out.

Now as he was speaking with me, I was in a deep sleep on my face toward the ground: but he touched me, and set me upright. – Daniel 8:18

As the appearance of the rainbow in the clouds on a rainy day, so was the appearance of the surrounding radiance. Such was the appearance of the likeness of the glory of the LORD. And when I saw it, I fell on my face. – Ezekiel 1:28

When I saw Him, I fell at His feet like a dead man. – John describing what happened when he saw God in Revelation 1:17

Unworthy sinner and fear… those are what it feels like to come into the physical presence of God. As we've seen, that's nothing like what *Jesus Always* describes.

We're Always In The presence of God

In the quote on the previous page John MacArthur makes an important point: God is always present. You are never out of God's presence. You cannot hide from God.

What we call "the presence of God" is not something that results from our entering into His presence. It has to do with our knowledge of God. As we know more about God, and see Him working, we then are more "aware" that God is always present and always active. It is our knowledge of God and His actions that we call "experiencing the presence" of God.

> *As you experience the range of human emotion in response to the Word of God, the Spirit of God uses those emotions to work on your heart. But, feeling God's presence doesn't exist. Because God can't be felt. He is a spirit. So when people say I felt the presence of the Lord, that's probably not an accurate representation of what they felt. They have felt convicted by the Word, or rejoice over the truth, nothing more than that is possible since you can't feel God.* - John MacArthur, Is a feeling of God's presence an indication of true worship? http://tinyurl.com/zcn2j36

WARNING: As with many other words, the New Age has co-opted the phrase "aware of god" such that it means one thing to a Christian and another to a New Ager. So we need to be careful with this phrase. Here is the difference.

The Bible – We become aware of God's presence as a result of reading scripture and God working in us or through us, or His actions being manifested in other ways. Our awareness of His presence comes as a result of knowledge and His actions.

New Age – We come aware of god's Presence within us by creating silence within us. The silence then allows us to "hear" god. Or we become aware of god's presence through a mystical experience that activates our feelings.

How Do We "Come Into" God's Presence Today?

You cannot come into God's presence, in the sense of truly being aware of God working in your life, unless you are a born-again Christian. If you are not born again, although you may feel close to god, your sin keeps you separated from God. Without the blood of Jesus what you are feeling is the presence of something, but it's not God. Only someone who is saved can experience the true presence of God.

> *"We not only have to come through Him—we must also realize that we come through His broken body and through His shed blood. Only one living way has been made for us, and that is the way upon the cross on Calvary's hill. The only thing that brings us into the presence of God, says the author of the Epistle to the Hebrews, is 'the bood of*

Jesus' (10:19)." - - Seeking The Face of God, Martyn Lloyd-Jones, US Edition 2005, page 45

As I mentioned, the book of Esther is an interesting book. It's a story of God's presence. The entire Jewish nation is about to be exterminated as the centuries long battle between the Agagites and Israel comes to a culmination. As the story progresses we see God rescue Israel through a series of providential actions. However God is never mentioned in this book. Why?

The main characters in the story are secular Jews. They have no relationship with God. The result is they are not experiencing the presence of God—and this is represented by God not being mentioned in this book. God is still present and active, but non-believers are not aware of His presence.

How does this compare with entering the presence of Jesus as described in *Jesus Always*? Here are a few examples from the February 3rd *Jesus Always* devotion.

> *"Let My Joyous Presence envelop you—permeating you through and through. As you delight in My nearness, time seems to slow down—enhancing your enjoyment of Me."*
>
> *"Speak My Name to remind yourself I am near, ready to help you."*
>
> *"Come freely into My loving Presence, letting your heart rejoice in Me."*
>
> *"As My follower, you can whisper, speak, or sing My Name with confidence that I am listening. This draws you closer to Me and helps you find strength in My Presence."*

None of these statements are Biblical. They are all New Age mysticism. For example, nowhere in scripture are we ever told to speak or whisper the name of Jesus in order to draw closer to Him. Scripture never tells us to let His Presence envelope us like a warm mist as described by Sarah Young in the introduction to *Jesus Calling*. These are mystical New Age practices. Don't get involved with these!

What does scripture say? How do we become aware of the presence of Jesus?

1. By repenting and trusting Jesus Christ as your savior.

2. By reading and studying His word in Scripture (knowledge).

3. Through obedience (righteousness and service).

Compare the *Jesus Always* quotes with what Martin Lloyd Jones writes about the presence of God:

> *"The real desire of his heart, and he puts it therefore in this expressive language, is, 'My soul thirsteth for God… my flesh longeth for thee.' The whole man is involved; there is nothing about him that is not, in this way, longing and thirsting for the presence of God.*
>
> *This is always a mark of the children of God. The desire for an intimate knowledge of God the Father is the biggest and most important thing in their lives; it is of greater importance to them than anything else whatsoever, and therefore they are more concerned about it than anything else."* – Martyn Lloyd-Jones, Seeking The Face of God, **US Edition 2005**, pages 105-106

Did you notice what he said? He says that a believer's whole person desires God's presence. And how does he describe this desire? It is a desire for an intimate **knowledge** of God. The presence of God and knowledge of God are directly linked. Why? If you don't know God, you have no way to recognize His presence. The better you know Him, the more you will be aware of His presence.

Do you long for a deep, intimate knowledge of God? That type of knowledge does not come from a mystical experience. It does not come from whispering Jesus' name, and trying to let the Presence of Jesus envelop you. It can only come from knowing scripture, and thus knowing God.

OBEDIENCE (righteousness and service)

There is a second part to being aware of the presence of God. You must put your knowledge into action. If you are not obeying scripture, you are not believing scripture. And if you do not believe scripture, you do not know God.

Obeying scripture is called righteousness. When we think of righteousness we often think of obeying the moral law, such as the Ten Commandments. And that is part of righteousness. The Ten Commandments describe God's character, and as bearers of God's image, we are to reflect His character.

Reflecting God's character means you are to love God and love your neighbor. That means you are to help others with their true needs. Through service to others you will more vividly be aware of the presence of God as He works in you and through you, as well as directly impacting the lives of others, as you serve others.

If you love Me, you will keep My commandments. – John 14:5

He who has My commandments and keeps them is the one who loves Me; and he who loves Me will be loved by My Father, and I will love him and will disclose Myself to him. – John 14:21

If you keep My commandments, you will abide in My love; just as I have kept My Father's commandments and abide in His love. – John 15:10

CHAPTER 10
WHAT KEEPS US FROM GOD'S PRESENCE?

God may feel distant, even if I am a close friend of His. David, who was called "a man after God's own heart" even felt far from God at times. Many of the Psalms he wrote beg God to make His presence felt. ...I have found in my life that when God feels distant it is almost always because I am pushing Him away. My sin has driven a wedge between myself and Him. – Tim Challies, Day Fourteen – When God Seems Distant, http://tinyurl.com/354w5zx

Therefore repent and return, so that your sins may be wiped away, in order that times of refreshing may come from the presence of the Lord; - Acts 3:19

If I want to be in the presence of God, shouldn't I find out what it is that separates me from God? I can then avoid those things that separate me from God. That makes sense. But there's more. I have a couple of questions I think need answering: Why are there times when God seems far away? What if I've never felt close to God? Do Christians experience depression? So let's get some answers.

John Wesley's Story

John Wesley was ordained at the age of 22. In college he formed and led a holiness club and a serious Bible study group. He scheduled his time so that he prayed for a few minutes every hour.

His desire was to be obedient to God. He served others with zeal. He gave away every penny he could spare to help the poor. He visited the sick and poor in their homes. He regularly went to a nearby prison, distributing food and teaching them to read, and then to read the catechism. He set up a school, helping to pay the teacher's salary from his own pocket. What did Wesley and his Bible study group get for all the good they were doing? They were ridiculed, scoffed at, and held in contempt by other students. But Wesley persevered.

He traveled to the American colonies where he preached and shared the gospel. People were saved, trusting in Christ as their Savior. His prayers were considered as having power, because people saw God answer them.

But on the return trip his ship was caught in a major storm and Wesley was terrified. He noticed that a group of Moravians were not afraid. They were trusting God to protect them. Wesley realized they had something he didn't have… that he never had… the inner peace that Christians have… he was and had always been separated from God Wesley recognized that he, himself, was not saved. He was not a Christian!

On May 24th 1738, shortly after returning from his ministry in the colonies, while hearing a reading of Luther's Preface to Romans, at about quarter to 9 in the evening, John Wesley felt a change in his heart and he knew he was finally saved.

John Wesley's early life puts most Christians today to shame. Yet, as he freely admitted, he was not saved. We are fallen and are so easy to deceive. Do as scripture says, test yourself (2 Corinthians 13:5). If Wesley had died before 9 PM on May 24, 1738, in spite of all the "good" he had done, he would have heard Jesus say, "*I never knew you.*" (Matthew 7:23).

Sin Separates Us from God

I'm now going to reveal an important truth you will not read about in *Jesus Always*. It is a clear fact of scripture: sin separates us from God. None of the "good" works an unsaved person does brings them any closer to God. Praying, bible studies and going to church do not bring the unrepentant any closer to god. Quieting your mind and bathing yourself in the Peace of god does not bring you any closer to God. If you want to be close to God... if you want to become aware of the presence of Jesus, you need to deal with the problem of sin.

> *But your iniquities* [sin] *have made a separation between you and your God, And your sins have hidden His face from you so that He does not hear.* – Isaiah 59:2

> *These will pay the penalty of eternal destruction, away from the presence of the Lord and from the glory of His power.* – 2 Thessalonians 1:9

The only way the problem of sin can be solved is through the cross. It's very straightforward: if you have the same problem John Wesley had—you are not a born again Christian—you are living in sin and are separated from God.

> *Do not be amazed that I said to you, "You must be born again."* – John 3:7

I've met people who have said, *"I never want to be one of THOSE born again Christians."*

Yes, there are some born again Christians who do not act in a Christ-like manner. There are also many people calling themselves "born again Christians," when in fact they are not Christian at all. Jesus warns us that on judgment day there will be many people who stand before Him thinking they are Christians, and they will hear Jesus say, *"I never knew you."*

> **Many** *will say to Me on that day, "Lord, Lord, did we not prophesy in Your name, and in Your name cast out demons, and in Your name perform many miracles?" And then I will declare to them, "I never knew you; depart from Me, you who practice lawlessness."* – Matthew 7:22-23

Notice it's not just a few who will stand before Jesus thinking they are Christians, but MANY, and they will even present evidence to Jesus supposedly proving they are Christian... yet Jesus will say, *"I never knew you; depart from me."*

Back To Basics: What Does Born Again Mean?

The phrase "born again" literally means "born from above." Nicodemus (John 3:3-7) had a real need. He needed a change of his heart—a spiritual transformation. New birth, being born again, is an act of God whereby eternal life is imparted to the person who believes (2 Corinthians 5:17; Titus 3:5; 1 Peter 1:3; 1 John 2:29; 3:9; 4:7; 5:1-4, 18). John 1:12, 13 indicates that being "born again" also carries the idea of "becoming children of God" through trust in the name of Jesus Christ. – http://www.gotquestions.org/born-again.html

To be born again means that God has given you a new heart... a new attitude toward God, a new way of thinking, and a new life. You are, literally, not the same person you were before.

You are born again the moment you repent and trust in Jesus Christ as your Savior... recognizing that as the one and only God, Jesus is the only one who can save you.

I have been crucified with Christ; and it is no longer I who live, but Christ lives in me; and the life which I now live in the flesh I live by faith in the Son of God, who loved me and gave Himself up for me. – Galatians 2:20

Those who are not born again are separated from God by their sin. That's not good. So let's deal with this problem. If you are truly a born again Christian what I'm about to say will match perfectly with what you believe. It you disagree with any of the following, you may be a Matthew 7 "Christian" and you need to repent and place your trust in Jesus alone.

Back to Basics: Sin Is The Problem

First you need to know you are a sinner. When I ask people on the street the question, *"Why should God let you into heaven?"* the most common answer is, *"Because I'm a good person."* (See the Good Person Test at: www.911Christ.com). But is that true? Are you truly a good person? Scripture says no, you are not!

For all have sinned and fall short of the glory of God. - Romans 3:23
Who is a sinner? The word Paul uses is "all." We all are sinners.

The way to know yourself a sinner is not to compare yourself with other people; it is to come face to face with the Law of God. Well, what is God's Law? Thou shalt not kill, thou shalt not steal? "I have never done that, therefore I am not a sinner." But, my friend, that is not the Law of God in its entirety. Would you like to know what the Law of God is? Here it is– "Thou shalt love the Lord thy God with all thy heart, and with all thy soul and with all thy mind and with all thy strength: this is the first commandment. And the second is like, namely this, Thous shalt love thy neighbor as thyself" (Mark 12:30,31 KJV). Forget all about drunkards and their like, forget all the people you read about in the press at the present time. Here is the test for you and me: Are you loving God with all your being? If you are not, you are sinner. - Martin Lloyd-Jones, Spiritual Depression, Its Causes and Cure, 1965, page 30

Martyn Lloyd-Jones talks about loving God. What does it mean "to love God?" Jesus is not talking about a feeling. To love God means to obey Him. That's why in Matthew 7 when Jesus tells the false Christians to depart from Him, He gives the reason as being because they practice lawlessness:

I never knew you; depart from Me, **you who practice lawlessness.** – Matthew 7:23

To be practicing lawlessness means you are not obeying Jesus and you do not love Jesus. Obedience to God and loving God are one and the same in scripture.

If you love Me, you will keep My commandments. – John 14:14

He who has My commandments and keeps them is the one who loves Me; - John 14:21

But, I just said that we all disobey God, we are all sinners. That means we are all heading for hell... turned away by Jesus with the words, *"I never knew you."*

<u>SHOULD YOU RUN FROM *JESUS ALWAYS?*</u>

But Wait! There is Good News!

Two thousand years ago Jesus died on the cross. But, He did more than dying physically. God poured out His full wrath on Jesus for everything you've done wrong... for every way and every time you've disobeyed God... in the past, present and future You have earned the penalty of God's wrath, and. Jesus has fully paid that penalty on your behalf.

If you believe this is true, and you repent (turn away from disobeying Jesus), trusting that Jesus has truly paid your penalty for disobeying Him in full, then your debt is paid and you will enter heaven free from sin.

If you do not believe Jesus died on the cross to pay your penalty for sin... if you do not trust that Jesus paid it all... then you must pay your penalty for sin yourself. That penalty is eternity in hell under the wrath of God.

So how do you know this is true? How do you know there truly is life after physical death?

There is no doubt Jesus died on the cross. The Romans were experts at crucifixion. They knew their work and they did it well. Jesus was dead and buried, with the tomb guarded to prevent anyone from stealing the body.

But then... on the third day after his crucifixion, the tomb was empty. Jesus had risen. He is alive! For the next 40 days He walked with people, He talked with people. They touched His wounds. This was not something done in secret. There were hundreds of eye-witnesses. Jesus' resurrection proved everything He said is true. There is life after physical death, if you trust in Him to save you from the just penalty for your breaking Gods laws.

Are You Trusting Jesus? No? Do it Today.

"Have you ever realized who God is? Everything in connection with religion is about Him. Christ came into the world and died? Why? To bring us to God. It's all about God. It is not some comfortable feeling that you and I have to strive for; it is not having your body healed or a thousand and one other things. The whole object of Christ and His death upon the cross, His burial, and His resurrection is to bring us to God. And the ultimate test of our profession of the Christian faith is our thoughts about God, our attitude

in His presence, our reverence and godly fear because our God is a consuming fire." - Seeking The Face of God, Martyn Lloyd-Jones, US Edition 2005, pages 36-37

One final thought: is it possible to not be saved (not be a born again Christian) and still experience the presence of God? Yes, it is. The Book of Revelation describes non-Christians experiencing the presence of God. From powerful political leaders and generals, to the everyday man on the street, this is how they responded:

"Then the kings of the earth and the great men and the commanders and the rich and the strong and every slave and free man hid themselves in the caves and among the rocks of the mountains; and they said to the mountains and to the rocks, "Fall on us and **hide us from the presence of Him who sits on the throne***, and from the wrath of the Lamb; for the great day of their wrath has come, and who is able to stand?"* – Revelation 6:15-17

Non-Christians will experience the presence of God. They will experience God's wrath for sin and desperately try to hide from the presence of God.

Christians also experience the presence of God, but being aware of God's presence is limited by sin. Sin, even for believers, causes a separation from God. So how do believers deal with sin and draw closer to God? Through repentance and confession. Repent… turn away from sin. And confess your sin to God.

SHOULD YOU RUN FROM *JESUS ALWAYS*?

CHAPTER 11
WHY DOESN'T JESUS UNDERSTAND SCRIPTURE?
MAY 29TH

Let's take a few minutes to look at the words of "Jesus" in another *Jesus Always* devotion, the one for May 29th where "Jesus" says:

> **THANK ME JOYFULLY** for forgiving *all* your sins—past, present, and future; known and unknown. Forgiveness is your greatest need, and I have met that need perfectly—forever! I am *the eternal Life that was with the Father and has appeared to you.* – Jesus Always, May 29th

It really gets to me that a single word is italicized, "*all*." That indicates this word is quoted from the Bible. I'm sorry, but I can't help asking this… which verse is the source of this quote? The word "all" is not used (that I could find) in any of the four references at the bottom of the devotion. It is used over 4,500 times in the Bible. For this quote of the word "*all*," what is the context? (For those who don't see it, I'm being sarcastic. It's ridiculous to "quote" a single word.)

Okay, let's get to the important statement in this devotion. The phrase I want to start with is not a scripture quote. Notice that "Jesus" says:

> **Forgiveness is your greatest need…** - Jesus Always, May 29th

Is that true? Is forgiveness truly your greatest need? Let's first look at this from the perspective of the non-believer.

What is the Greatest Need of a Non-believer?

Our greatest need as a non-believer was for our debt for sin to be paid. We needed Jesus' work on the cross. When we repent and trust Jesus we receive everything else: salvation, forgiveness, justification, atonement, reconciliation, propitiation and regeneration.

Imagine you've broken into an expensive house, stolen everything of value, and totally destroyed everything else, including every family picture and video. And you not only killed the dog, you murdered the women and children living there. Unfortunately for you it was all recorded by a hidden security camera.

The police find you, and now you are in court. The judge gives the verdict… guilty. And then he says, "I forgive you." It turns out it was the judge's home and it was his family you murdered. And he forgives you. Amazing!

Does that mean you go free? No, of course not. You still must pay the penalty for what you've done wrong. Otherwise there is no justice. A judge, who lets a law-breaker go free, is not a good judge. Forgiveness does not eliminate the need for justice.

God is good judge. He is just. Yes, He offers forgiveness, but there also must be justice. The penalty for sin must be paid. A nonbeliever's greatest need is for the cross. Then, as a result of your penalty for sin being paid, you also receive forgiveness (and justification, and reconciliation, and regeneration, etc.).

What is a Believer's Greatest Need?

Jesus Always appears to have been written for believers, so let's look at this devotion from that perspective. With Jesus' death on the cross the penalty for all your sins has been paid and you are forgiven. The May 29th *Jesus Always* devotion says:

> Because you believe in Me as your Savior-God, you have *everlasting Life*. Let this amazing promise fill you with Joy (capital "J") and drive out fear of the future. – *Jesus Always*, May 29th

WHY DOESN'T JESUS UNDERSTAND SCRIPTURE? MAY 29th

Except for the capital "L" and "J," that's a true statement about the cross and the effect the cross has on our lives. So, if this is true, why is our greatest need still for forgiveness?

If our greatest need is for forgiveness, apparently there is some aspect of forgiveness we do not have as believers. But, "Jesus" says he has already perfectly met that need (see the quote at the beginning of the chapter). Okay… that's a little confusing. (Keep in mind 1 Corinthians 14:33, which states that God is not a God of confusion.)

What we are seeing here is something that is common in New Age teaching… statements that sound very good and spiritual, but when you actually try to understand what they say… it's nothing more than doublespeak.

Maybe if we list the actual information in the May 29th devotion we can make sense of this:

- **Forgiveness is your greatest need:** since it is a need, it is something you do not have, or maybe you do not have it in its fullness. Before we go to the next statement keep in mind this is Jesus speaking. Jesus is God. He is perfect, including being perfect in the specific words he uses. That means declarative statements, like the ones we are reading here, are to be taken literally.

- **I have met that need perfectly:** Jesus has fully met your need for forgiveness. So it is no longer a need. This contradicts the first statement which said forgiveness is our greatest need.

- **How can we know Jesus has "met that need perfectly?"** Because he is *"the eternal Life that was with the Father and has appeared to you."* (This is a paraphrase of 1 John 1:2.) What does that mean? Has Jesus actually appeared to you? If you believe in New Age theology, of course Jesus has appeared to you. Everything is Jesus (God) and Jesus is everything. But, if you believe in the Bible… no, Jesus has not appeared to you.

The paraphrasing used by *Jesus Always* has changed the meaning of 1 John 1:2. The word "you" at the end of the quote is the word "us" in the original text. In the original John is speaking. He is giving his credentials as an apostle by listing four ways, some of them multiple times; he has perceived the word of life with his physical senses. The four are highlighted in bold in the quote below. Here is what the original says, in its context:

> *That which was from the beginning, which* **we have heard, which we have seen with our eyes, which we have looked at and our hands have touched**—*this we proclaim concerning the Word of life. The life appeared;* **we have seen it** *and testify to it, and we proclaim to you the eternal life, which was with the Father and has* **appeared to us**. *We proclaim to you what we* **have seen and heard**, *so that you also may have fellowship with us.* - 1 John 1:1-3a NIV

John is saying, "You can trust what I say, and have fellowship with me, because I'm an eye-witness. I was there. I heard Jesus reveal the gospel (referred to here as "eternal life") with my own ears. When I testify about the word of life (Jesus), you can be confident it is the truth."

The way *Jesus Always* has paraphrased this verse makes "Jesus" say that you were an eye-witness to Jesus. Yes, that would make you very special, but Jesus (the word of life) has not appeared to you.

Yes, forgiveness was a need before you were saved. Yes, that need was met perfectly by Jesus through His death on the cross. But, if you are truly a believer in Jesus Christ as your savior, why is *Jesus Always* saying forgiveness is still your greatest need and promising something you already have? As I said, this devotion makes no sense.

Let's look at a couple of questions:

Do Believers Need Additional Forgiveness?

The answer is no. You have complete forgiveness of all your sins, past, present and future. As a believer forgiveness is not one of your needs ... you already have it. But, what about 1 John 1:9 in which John tells believers:

> *If we confess our sins, He is faithful and righteous to forgive us our sins and to cleanse us from all unrighteousness.*

What John is saying is that the characteristic of confessing sins is a defining characteristic of a believer. If you are someone who is confessing your sins to God, then you are someone who already has total forgiveness and the righteousness of God has already been given to you through the cross. John is not saying you need forgiveness and thus must confess your sins. He is saying that because you confess your sins, that action shows you were already forgiven when you became a believer.

> *What John is actually saying here about confession is that since believers are forgiven, they will regularly confess their sins, agreeing with God about sin— they acknowledge its reality and affirm that it is a transgression of His law and a violation of His will, the presence of which the truly penitent seek to eliminate from their lives. ... Stated another way, their forgiveness is not because of their ongoing confession, but their ongoing pattern of penitence and confession is because of their forgiveness and transformation.* - John MacArthur, New Testament Commentary, 1-3 John, 2007, page 39

What Is A Believer's Greatest Need?

It's time to get to the heart of the matter. *Jesus Always* says that, as a believer, forgiveness is your greatest need. What does scripture say?

Let's look at Paul's letters which contain many prayers for believers. If forgiveness was our greatest need, I'd think Paul would be praying for that need. I have all 42 of Paul's prayers compiled in a single Word document and printed out. (They take five pages.) I don't see that he asks for forgiveness for believers in any of them.

What Does Paul Pray For?

In Paul's prayers you see that he prays for the specific needs of various churches and people. For example, his prayers include asking God to provide increasing knowledge of God; to give discernment; and to give wisdom, unity, endurance, and righteousness. But he never prays for God to give forgiveness. If this was a believer's greatest need, you'd think it would show up in at least one of Paul's prayers for believers. But, it doesn't.

What are believer's greatest needs? It varies based on their situation. Here is a sampling of Paul's prayers:

Paul's prayer for the Ephesians:

I pray that the eyes of your heart may be enlightened, so that you will know what is the hope of His calling, what are the riches of the glory of His inheritance in the saints, and what is the surpassing greatness of His power toward us who believe. – Ephesians 1:18-19a

Paul's prayer for the Philippians:

And this I pray, that your love may abound still more and more in real knowledge and all discernment, so that you may approve the things that are excellent, in order to be sincere and blameless until the day of Christ. – Philippians 1:9-10

Paul's prayer for the Colossians:

For this reason also, since the day we heard of it, we have not ceased to pray for you and to ask that you may be filled with the knowledge of His will in all spiritual wisdom and understanding, so that you will walk in a manner worthy of the Lord, to please Him in all respects, bearing fruit in every good work and increasing in the knowledge of God. – Colossians 1:9-10

Paul's prayer for the Thessalonians:

May the Lord cause you to increase and abound in love for one another, and for all people, just as we also do for you; so that He may establish your hearts without blame in holiness before our God and Father at the coming of our Lord Jesus with all His saints. – 1 Thessalonians 3:12-13

Paul mentions the need for knowledge in three of these four prayers, but forgiveness is never mentioned. Either he is totally unaware of a believer's need for forgiveness, or *Jesus Always* got it wrong. Who are you going to believe? Paul or *Jesus Always*? (I chose Paul.) This is becoming very irritating. The "Jesus" of *Jesus Always* just does not understand scripture. And I'm not looking for the worst of the devotions. These are basically random devotions.

P.S. – I wasn't going to mention this, but *Jesus Always* again contradicts itself. We've been talking about the May 29th devotion saying our greatest need is forgiveness. BUT, I just happened to notice that in the August 9th devotion "Jesus" says: *"I know what you need most: to be still in My Presence. Take some deep breaths, and fix your gaze on Me."* (That sounds like New Age practicing the Presence.) So which is it? What do we need most? If it is forgiveness, we should be repenting, and turning to Jesus as our Savior. If it is the New Age feeling and experience of the Presence of Jesus, then we should be sitting in stillness and using New Age practices to come into the Presence of "Jesus." Come on Jesus, make up your mind.

P.S. Again – Here is yet another one, May 9th… *"Your deepest need is to lean on, trust in, and be confident in Me."* So, which of these is what we most need? Forgiveness? To be still in His Presence? Or to "lean on, trust in, and be confident in Me?" How can you even consider trusting this confused and contradictory "Jesus" to teach you?

A Jesus who contradicts himself IS NOT the Jesus of the bible!

CHAPTER 13
TRUE JOY:
WHAT DOES SCRIPTURE SAY?

True joy is a gift from God to those who believe the gospel, being produced in them by the Holy Spirit as they receive and obey the Word, mixed with trials, and set their hope on future glory. –
John MacArthur sermon: The Epistle of Joy
http://tinyurl.com/jobs2gn

Christian joy is a good feeling in the soul, produced by the Holy Spirit, as he causes us to see the beauty of Christ in the Word and in the world.
– John Piper, How Do You Define Joy?
http://tinyurl.com/hkzhusp

The emotion evoked by well-being, success, or good fortune or by the prospect of possessing what one desires. A state of happiness or felicity. -
Merriam-Webster Dictionary

The subtitle for *Jesus Always* is *"Finding Joy in His Presence."* This is a book about joy. In this chapter we are going to talk about true joy and learn about the source of true joy. Compare what you read in the next few chapters (summarized as: believe, have the fruit of the Spirit, receive and obey God's word, experience trials, and set your hope on future glory) with *Jesus Always* (summarized as: having good thoughts and experiencing the Presence of Jesus and sparkles of joy).

Before we talk about the Biblical source of joy, it might be a good idea to define what we are talking about. I've noticed differences in the above quotes, primarily between the secular definition (Meriam-Webster Dictionary), and the definition given by the two Christians.

Both John MacArthur and John Piper describe joy as a gift from God produced by the Holy Spirit. They base their definitions on scripture, describing joy as one of the fruits of the Spirit (Galatians 5:22-23). This is the joy we are talking about.

> *But the fruit of the Spirit is love, joy, peace, patience, kindness, goodness, faithfulness, gentleness, self-control; against such things there is no law. Now those who belong to Christ Jesus have crucified the flesh with its passions and desires.* - Galatians 5:22-24

Are Joy and Happiness The Same?

For our purposes we're going to make a distinction between joy and happiness. Happiness is the result of your circumstances. For example, being with a special person results in your being happy. When you are not with that person, you may not as happy. When *Jesus Always* talks about Joy" in most cases it is actually talking about happiness... a good feeling that comes from your present circumstances.

Joy, on the other hand, is a gift of the Holy Spirit and is unrelated to your circumstances. For an example let's look at Acts 16:

> *"But about midnight Paul and Silas were praying and singing hymns of praise to God..."* – Acts 16:25

It seems that Paul and Silas were having a good time together. They were staying up late enjoying each other's fellowship as they prayed and sang hymns of praise together. What were their circumstances? Let's jump back a few verses and find out:

> *The crowd rose up together against them* [Paul and Silas], *and the chief magistrates tore their robes off them and proceeded to order them to be beaten with rods. When they had struck them with many blows, they threw them into prison, commanding the jailer to guard them securely; and he, having received such a command, threw them into the inner prison and fastened their feet in the stocks.* - Acts 14:22-24

They had been beaten, probably rather severely, with many blows. If you had been beaten as they had, you'd probably be in the emergency room demanding pain killers. But, there was no medical treatment for Paul and Silas. They were put into prison, which in those days were dark, foul, filthy places. In addition, their feet where fastened in stocks. Stocks would hold your feet and legs motionless so that your muscles cramped up causing serious pain.

So Paul and Silas had been severely beaten, were in serious pain, locked in a dark, damp cave-like prison, with their legs cramping up. Not what I'd call the best of circumstances... yet they were filled with joy, singing hymns and praising God. Why?

Their focus was on the cross and their joy was a gift of the Holy Spirit. A gift given to all believers. Their circumstance could not take away their joy. All Christians have this joy available… always… in all circumstances… because all Christians have the fruit of the Spirit.

But I Don't Feel Like I'm Filled With Joy

What if you don't feel joy? Is it because you are not a Christian? Or maybe it is because you've moved out of the presence of Jesus, as *Jesus Always* implies. No. If you are a true believer, you have all of the fruits of the Spirit available, including joy.[6]

> *...neither death, nor life, nor angels, nor principalities, nor things present, nor things to come, nor powers, nor height, nor depth, nor any other created thing, will be able to separate us from the love of God, which is in Christ Jesus our Lord.* – Romans 8:38-39

So, why would you not be experiencing the joy scripture promises?

Joy is a gift to believers from the Holy Spirit. The #1 reason people are not experiencing joy is that they think they are a Christian, but in reality they are not.

So am I saying you are a false Christian? No. true Christians can also have times when they are not experiencing the fullness of the joy

---

17 - We can choose to be grumpy (not have joy). We always have the ability to choose, including to choose to be joyous or not. That's why throughout the New Testament we are commanded to be joyous. Keep in mind, God would not command us to do something we could not do... something in which we had no choice about. So, choose to be filled with joy!

they have in Christ. We'll talk about that in the next two chapters. But first, let's start at the beginning with our foundation.

To have joy, you must have the Holy Spirit, meaning you are a true believer. So, if it seems you are not experiencing joy, the first thing to do is check your foundation, test yourself to see if you are in the faith. (2 Corinthians 13:5)

But wait, isn't there a third option? What if you are saved, but you don't have the Holy Spirit.

Can You Be Saved and Not Have the Holy Spirit?

This is a serious question. What if someone is saved, so they are a born again believer, but they do not have the Holy Spirit? That would mean they don't have the fruit of the Spirit. Could that be why they do not have joy?

Scripture does not allow that possibility. The moment you are saved, you have the Holy Spirit. You do not need to speak in tongues, nor do you need to be baptized, nor do you need to do or say anything else. The Holy Spirit indwells all Christians the moment they are saved. Romans 8:9 says: if you do not have the Spirit, you are not saved.[7]

> *However, you are not in the flesh but in the Spirit, if indeed the Spirit of God dwells in you. But if anyone does not have the Spirit of Christ, he does not belong to Him.* – Romans 8:9

But, doesn't scripture talk about the Holy Spirit being removed from some people, such as David in Psalm 51? Yes, it does. But, there is a difference between Old Testament times and New Testament times. In a Q&A session John MacArthur described the difference between the indwelling of the Holy Spirit in Old Testament times vs. the church age:

> *Before the inauguration of the church, the Holy Spirit would come upon certain individuals, such as prophets and national leaders, to empower them for the special tasks God gave them. But Jesus introduced the indwelling*

---

18 - If you are asking, "What about Acts 8:12?" A proper answer to that question requires more space that I have available here. Please go to the "Web Exclusives" menu on our web site for the answer: www.NotJesusAlways.com

ministry of the Holy Spirit in the life of every believer. Every believer who is part of the church enjoys the permanent indwelling of the Holy Spirit (cf. Romans 8:9).

This explains what we read in Psalm 51:11. David's cry to God not to remove His Spirit from him did not refer to a permanent indwelling of the Spirit but to the special filling of the Spirit God granted to enable him to serve effectively as Israel's king. http://tinyurl.com/huzm4wx

The Holy Spirit indwells all true believers, sealing (protecting) believers such that no one and nothing can take away their salvation, and that means no one can take away your joy.

In Him, you also, after listening to the message of truth, the gospel of your salvation—having also believed, you were sealed in Him with the Holy Spirit of promise, who is given as a pledge of our inheritance, with a view to the redemption of God's own possession, to the praise of His glory. – Ephesians 1:13-14

Since joy is a gift from the Holy Spirit, and all believers have the Holy Spirit, if you are not feeling joy, might it be a good idea to check your foundation, and test yourself to see if you are in the faith? In other words, shouldn't you do what scripture commands you to do?

Test yourselves to see if you are in the faith; examine yourselves! – 2 Corinthians 13:5

I can put it, finally, like this: the ultimate cause of all spiritual depression is unbelief. – D. Martyn Lloyd-Jones, Spiritual Depression: Its Causes and Cure, 1965, page 20

About five years ago I was experiencing some minor pain in my chest whenever I inhaled. It was no big deal and I mostly ignored it, figuring it would go away. Then one day it became a very sharp chest pain, just about knocking me off my feet. My wife called 911. An ambulance came. Fire trucks came. Our little street was packed with emergency vehicles.

On the ride to the hospital the paramedics keep feeding me aspirin. They kept asking if I had any left arm pain. "Nope. No pain in my arms," was my answer.

I was whisked into the emergency room and they did all kinds of tests... taking blood... hooking me up to wires... EKG, ECG and some kind of scan I didn't recognize. All of this was done to check the condition of my heart.

After a while they checked me into a regular room. This was going to be an overnight stay. I needed to be monitored and additional heart related tests needed to be done the next day.

The next day they wanted to rerun some of the tests. Both my wife and I objected. The bits and pieces I was hearing about the test results were not adding up. So the doctor consulted with another doctor. A third doctor was brought in, and the diagnosis was... pleurisy. That's an inflammation of the lining around the lung that causes pain... and it was the correct diagnosis. What was the cure? Give it time. It would heal. And it did.

My heart was fine. Was I upset about all the fuss and tests they did? Did I think it was all a waste of time? Not at all. I was impressed. Chest pain is serious, and the appropriate tests are called for. If I had a heart problem, diagnosing it quickly was essential. I'm blessed to live in a place where this type of medical care is available.

So now we come to the command in scripture to test yourself to see if you are in the faith. This command angers some people... and those are usually the ones who turn out not to be saved. But testing yourself is important. A potential heart attack is serious, and as I found out the testing is extensive. But, if you have not received a new heart from God, and you are not truly born again, you are facing serious consequences that are eternal. This is so critically important that we should rejoice that spiritual tests are available, as I did about the medical tests.

By the way, these are not tests created by man. Scripture commands us to test ourselves, and it provides those tests.

Test Yourselves to See if You Are in the Faith

As we begin the testing process let's keep Matthew 7 in mind. The things we do, our works, are not necessarily what demonstrate we are Christians:

"Not everyone who says to Me, 'Lord, Lord,' will enter the kingdom of heaven, but he who does the will of My Father who is in heaven will enter. Many will say to Me on that day, 'Lord, Lord, did we not prophesy in Your name, and in Your name cast out demons, and in Your name perform many miracles?' And then I will declare to them, 'I never knew you; depart from Me, you who practice lawlessness.'" – Matthew 7:21-23

These are Jesus' words. Words you NEVER want to hear, *"I never knew you."*

Even people who prophesied in Jesus' name... people who cast out demons... and even people who have done miracles in the name of Jesus'... these are people who were sure they were heading for heaven and they had the actions in their life to prove it. But, what does Jesus say to them? *"I never knew you."*

These are people who were confident they knew Jesus, but Jesus said, *"I never knew you."* Those are chilling words.

Jesus makes it clear that there will be MANY people who think they are Christians, but they are not. For example, He tells the story of the wheat and the tares:

Jesus presented another parable to them, saying, "The kingdom of heaven may be compared to a man who sowed good seed in his field. But while his men were sleeping, his enemy came and sowed tares among the wheat, and went away. But when the wheat sprouted and bore grain, then the tares became evident also. The slaves of the landowner came and said to him, 'Sir, did you not sow good seed in your field? How then does it have tares?' And he said to them, 'An enemy has done this!' The slaves *said to him, 'Do you want us, then, to go and gather them up?' But he said, 'No; for while you are gathering up the tares, you may uproot the wheat with them. Allow both to grow together until the harvest; and in the time of the harvest I will say to the reapers, "First gather up the tares and bind them in bundles to burn them up; but gather the wheat into my barn."'' - Matthew 13:24-30

A "tare" is a weed that looks just like wheat, until it matures. Jesus is saying there will be tares in the church, false converts that appear to be true Christians. Not only do the false Christians not know they are unsaved, they appear to others to be true Christians. You can't tell the difference.

What is The "Test" Scripture Talks About?

There are tests all throughout scripture. For example, the Beatitudes describe a true Christian (see my book, *Happy Are The...*) allowing you to compare yourself with the ideal Jesus describes. For example, do you mourn over sin and do you hunger and thirst for righteousness... meaning do you hunger and thirst to be free from sin?

Another option is 1st John. John wrote this letter to help Christians have assurance of their faith. It describes ten characteristics of a true believer in Christ.

So let's take a test. Based on scripture here are five points, compiled by John MacArthur, that characterize a true Christian. Do not be discouraged if you fail in some points. We all do. No one is perfect. What you should look for are trends. Are you improving in each of these areas?

#1 - Are you experiencing a growing knowledge of, and turning from sin?

Do you mourn over your sin? Do you run from sin? (1 Corinthians 6:18) Do you acknowledge (confess) your sin to God? (1 John 1:7-10 and Romans 7:24). Are there things you did that where acceptable several years ago, but now you know are sinful and you have stopped doing them? Are you more serious about avoiding sin now than you were two years ago? These are signs of a Christian.

On the other hand, do you sometimes do wrong things and excuse them with reasons such as: you've been mistreated by others, or you had a childhood trauma? Do you feel you lack of self-esteem and that's why you occasionally cheat, lie, or steal? Do you feel you could be a good person, if only your circumstances were somehow changed?

Test #1 Summary

If you understand the problem is sin... if you have a growing knowledge of sin... if things you did two years ago seemed okay then, but now you know they were sinful... then you've passed the first test.

If you think you are good person, or that we all have little sin in our lives and God loves us and will just forgive us… if you think sin is not important; if you blame your sin on someone else, or on your circumstances, or make other excuses for continuing in sin, then you fail the first test.

#2 - Do you desire what is right and pure?

Do you have a deep longing to obey the commands of God? Do you desire to correctly understand scripture? Do you want to change the way you think, replacing your desire for sin with a desire for righteousness? Do other people see a distinct difference in you now compared to what you were like before you began trusting in Jesus?

Or, do you behave well and speak in kind words when others can see and hear you, but your true desires are for sin? That is called external righteousness. It's a "show" put on for others.

Jesus taught that it's what is inside us that is important. The world sees the outside; God sees what's inside, including your thoughts and motives.

Many people take their desires and make them the standard of what is right or wrong. They redefine what the Bible says so that certain behaviors are no longer defined as sinful. Common examples include: sex outside of marriage, looking at pornography, homosexuality, and downloading pirated music from the internet.

The Christian, on the other hand, studies scripture to gain a better and true understanding of how God (not culture) defines right and wrong.

Test #2 Summary

If your desire is to obey God... to truly know God's desires and bring your life into alignment with God's desires... and to know His desires the way He defines them, not the way our culture defines them, then you've passed the second test.

If you are not concerned about how God defines right and wrong. Or there are some of God's commands you believe do not apply in today's culture, or maybe they don't apply to you, then you've failed test number two.

#3 - Are you submissive to divine authority?

Are you a willing servant (Luke 11:25-35)? Do you submit to the authority of scripture? Is your desire to understand what the original author intended? (Instead of your understanding of scripture being influenced by our current culture.) Are you open to rebuke and correction from other Christians?

Or, do you believe scripture needs to be understood in light of our culture? Is your understanding of scripture significantly different than the historical understanding of scripture? Was the Holy Bible written by people who did not have the science and understanding of human psychology we now have, and so they got some things wrong?

Test #3 Summary

If you are submitting to the authority of scripture, taking the plain meaning of the words of scripture, and you are open to correction and rebuke from other Christians (as commanded by scripture), then you've passed the third test.

If you believe that our understanding of scripture must be based on science, human psychology, or that it must be updated to conform to a cultural context, then you've failed the third test.

#4 - Do you obey God?

This fourth test is very simple: is your desire to obey God, and when you sin do you mourn over your disobedience? (Luke 6:46; John 8:31; John 14:15, 23-24; 15:10; 1 John 2:3-5; 3:24; 52-3)

Test #4 Summary

If your desire is to obey God, and you read the scriptures to learn what He says, (if your focus is on being better able to obey God), then you've passed the fourth test.

If you desire to be accepted by the world (be accepted in the culture), or you desire what you want for yourself (your focus is on yourself), then you've failed the fourth test.

#5 - Do you have love for God, for Christians, and Other People?

Do you understand that love and obedience to God are the same? To love God is to obey God (1 John 5:2). To obey God is to love God. Have you studied scripture so you know how God defines love? (1 Corinthians 13:1-7, Romans 12:1-2; 9-21)

Are there Christians whom you avoid or hate? (1 John 2:9-11)? Do you have an unresolved conflict with a Christian brother or sister?

Test #5 Summary - The Biblical Definition of Love

Is Biblical love a feeling? Do you define love as being like a warm puppy, a happy baby, or a spouse you feel close to? Is love an overwhelming desire to be with someone? Can you fall into love... and fall out of love? The answer to all of these is, "no."

If you understand that to love God is to obey God... if you understand agape love as sacrificially meeting the real needs (not wants) of other people, without regard to whether you like them. If you understand that the greatest need people have is to repent and trust Jesus as their Lord and Savior, then you've passed the fifth test.

If there are Christians you hate, or with whom you have an unresolved conflict... If you understand love as a feeling, and in particular a feeling that can come and go... then you've failed the fifth test.

The Finally Summary

None of us gets a perfect score on this five point test. We all probably fail in one or more area. However, the key question is what is your heart attitude? Are you trying to improve? Is your desire to improve? Are you actually improving? Are you doing better this year than two years ago?

Another way to look at it is, do you know what the problem is? And then do you know the solution to the problem... the only solution to the problem? Fill in the blanks:

The problem is _____.

The solution is: _____ and _____.

Has the solution changed your life? Has your behavior changed? Are you literally a different person since the solution was implemented in your life?

The Answers:

The problem is sin.

The solution is: repent and trust Jesus. Trust that Jesus Christ has fully paid the penalty you've earned for disobeying God. And know that He rose from the dead, proving everything He said is true… there is life after death! Once you've done this, then the door is open to truly experiencing joy. This is a fact never mentioned in *Jesus Always*.

When you repented and trusted Christ, God have you a new heart and made you a new person. This results in a significant change in how you think and act. You are a different person. The change is so significant that others will be see this change in you.

CHAPTER 14
TRUE JOY:
THE SOURCE OF A BELIEVER'S JOY

In the previous chapter we dealt with the question of false converts. Those who are not truly saved and thus they do not have the Holy Spirit. It is impossible for them to experience the joy that is one of the fruits of the Holy Spirit.

What about believers? Are there times when believers are not experiencing joy? The answer is yes. Does that mean they've lost their salvation? No. Does that mean they've lost the Holy Spirit? No. Then what's the problem?

Let's look at the John MacArthur quote that opened the previous chapter:

> *"True joy is a gift from God to those who believe the gospel, being produced in them by the Holy Spirit as they receive and obey the Word, mixed with trials, and set their hope on future glory."* – John MacArthur sermon: The Epistle of Joy
> http://tinyurl.com/jobs2gn

MacArthur gives four criteria that are necessary for joy:
- Believe the gospel (you are saved). I discussed this in the previous chapter.
- Receive and obey the Word
- A proper response to trials.
- Set your hope on future glory.

Compare this with one of Sarah Young's favorite devotions, September 5th. Both MacArthur and Young talk about having joy. Yet what they say has little in common. One is giving you the truth, the other is deceiving you.

In this chapter we'll learn about Christians who are not experiencing joy. The first bullet point above is to be a believer. I'm assuming you are, so let's look at the next point on MacArthur's list.

Receive and Obey the Word

What separates you from God? Sin. If you are not receiving and obeying the Word of God, you are sinning. Sin separates you from God and thus from joy.

Sin is very appealing. It promises happiness and joy, however it does not deliver on those promises. When David saw Bathsheba bathing on her rooftop, David sinned. He lusted after her. Then his desire for sinful "pleasure" resulted in his committing adultery with her. And he went further. His desire to hide his sin resulted in his murdering Uriah the Hittite. David's life was never the same after that. He was still a man after God's own heart, but his sin took his joy.

If you are not experiencing the joy of the Lord, look for sin in your life, repent, and confess it to God, and your joy will grow.

Proper Response to Trials

Scriptures does not say to go out and find ways to put yourself into a circumstance in which you are experiencing trials. You don't need to look for them, you will experience trials... some large and many that are small.

What do you do with your trials? Grumble and complain, and make everyone around you as miserable as you are? Or do you respond with joy, trusting God, realizing that God is in control and will supply all of your needs:

> *Count it all joy, my brothers, when you meet trials of various kinds, for you know that the testing of your faith produces steadfastness. And let steadfastness have its full effect, that you may be perfect and complete, lacking in nothing. If any of you lacks wisdom, let him ask God, who gives*

generously to all without reproach, and it will be given him. But let him ask in faith, with no doubting, for the one who doubts is like a wave of the sea that is driven and tossed by the wind. - James 1:2-8

What do you do when you are overwhelmed with trials? When everything seems to be going wrong? Do you praise God, thanking Him for the opportunity to trust in Him? That is the Biblical response:

Rejoice in hope, be patient in tribulation, be constant in prayer. - Romans 12:12

No temptation has overtaken you that is not common to man. God is faithful, and he will not let you be tempted beyond your ability, but with the temptation he will also provide the way of escape, that you may be able to endure it. - 1 Corinthians 10:13

What do you do when certain individuals target you, causing you nothing put problems… and they won't stop? Do you seek retaliation and vengeance, or do you love them and serve them?

If your enemy is hungry, give him food to eat;
And if he is thirsty, give him water to drink;
For you will heap burning coals on his head,
And the LORD *will reward you.* - Proverbs 25-21-22

How you respond to trials and difficulties impacts your joy or lack of joy. When you respond in love, trusting God, your joy will grow.

Set Your Hope On Future Glory.

If you ever get the chance, read the book "*The Heavenly Man*" by Brother Yun. It is the story of a Chinese Pastor who refuses to stop preaching God's truth. As a result he is regularly put in prison where he is beaten and tortured. Chinese prisons are not pleasant places, yet Brother Yun still has joy. Why? Because his eyes were constantly on his hope of future glory.

When scripture says "hope" that does not mean something unsure. It is not referring to something that may or may not happen.

MacArthur explains what hope means in an article titled, "A Mystery Manifested:"

> *That Christ indwell-s all believers is the source for their hope of glory and is the subject or theme of the gospel ministry. What makes the gospel attractive is not just that it promises present joy and help, but that it promises eternal honor, blessing, and glory. When Christ comes to live in a believer, His presence is the anchor of the promise of heaven—the guarantee of future bliss eternally (cf. 2 Cor. 5:1–5; Eph. 1:13–14).* - John MacArthur, A Mystery Manifested, http://tinyurl.com/hnk2t8o

These are the source of your joy: salvation, obedience, proper response to trials and difficulties, and keeping your eyes on the future glory. How does this compare with *Jesus Always'* promise of his "continual Presence" and that you should keep looking for that Presence until *"you can discern the Light of My Presence shining upon your difficulties, reflecting sparkles of Joy back to you?"*

Jesus Always and Biblical truth are very different. Which one are you going follow?

CHAPTER 15
DEPRESSION & THE FRUIT OF THE SPIRIT

"True joy is a gift from God to those who believe the gospel, being produced in them by the Holy Spirit as they receive and obey the Word, mixed with trials, and set their hope on future glory." – John MacArthur sermon: The Epistle of Joy (http://www.gty.org/resources/sermons/50-1/the-epistle-of-joy)

You've tested yourself, you have truly repented and are trusting in Jesus alone as your Savior. According to scripture you should be experiencing the fruits of the Spirit, the second of which is joy:

> *But the fruit of the Spirit is love, joy, peace, patience, kindness, goodness, faithfulness, gentleness, self-control; against such things there is no law. Now those who belong to Christ Jesus have crucified the flesh with its passions and desires.* - Galatians 5:22-24

But you are not particularly feeling very joyful,. And you haven't felt joy for a long time. What's wrong? Is it because you are not saved and the test did not reveal this? Do you have sin in your life? Are you fighting against numerous trials? Or is there some other problem?

This is a complex question. First you need to be sure you are not confusing a lack of happiness with a lack of joy. There are going to be times when we are not happy. Happiness, and unhappiness, are both emotions. Like other emotions they are a gift God has given us to help motivate us to action or inaction.

Let's say you've just lost your job and you are very unhappy. That unhappiness motivates you to get up off the couch and go out to look for a new job. So in this case, the emotion of unhappiness provides a positive motivation.

But, what if what you are feeling is more than unhappiness? It is a persistent depression. Christians do get depressed. Great Christian leaders, such as D. Martyn Lloyd-Jones and Charles Spurgeon experienced depression:

> *Spurgeon was indeed frequently "in heaviness." Sometimes Spurgeon's depression was the direct result of his various illnesses, perhaps simply psychologically, and in the case of his gout, probably physiologically as well. Despite this, Spurgeon thought of his own depression as his "worst feature" and once commented that "despondency is not a virtue; I believe it is a vice."*
> -- The Anguish and Agonies of Charles Spurgeon, Christianity Today, Issue 29, 1991

This is not a topic *Jesus Always* provides any help with, but it is real and it is serious.

Depression is not always a spiritual issue. It can be caused by physical illness, or other physiological problems. That's why the first step to take, if you are persistently feeling depressed, is to see your family physician. They will check for organic, chemical, and physical causes of the depression. Once those are eliminated, then you can look for spiritual causes.

How do You Deal with Spiritual Depression?

In a booklet titled *"What Do You Do When You Become Depressed?"* (R&R Publishing, www.prpbooks.com, phone 800-631-0094) the founder of Nouthetic (Biblical) Counseling, Jay Adams, writes:

> *Although depression is a terribly debilitating problem that is far too widespread among Christians as well as among those who do not know God, it is not so difficult a problem to solve as it might first seem to be.*

And what is the solution? To know the solution you need to know the cause. John MacArthur reveals the cause:

DEPRESSION AND THE FRUIT OF THE SPIRIT

> *Although it is a gift from God to every believer and administered by the Holy Spirit (Galatians 5:22), joy is not always constant and full (cf. 1 John 1:4). The only certain cause for loss of joy in a believer's life is sin, which corrupts his fellowship with the Lord, who is the source of joy. Such sinful attitudes as dissatisfaction, bitterness, sullenness, doubt, fear and negativism cause joy to be forfeited. Consequently, the only way to restore lost joy is to repent and return to proper worship of and obedience to God.* – John MacArthur, New Testament Commentary, Philippians, 2001, page 56.

The following is a summation of the recommendations Jay Adams gives in his booklet. Notice that Adams also focuses on turning from sin and toward obeying God. (Compare these Biblical instructions for having joy with what Sarah Young writes in *Jesus Always*. She totally ignores the effects of sin.)

1. *Confess your sin of failing to assume your responsibilities, along with any other sin that you may have failed to confess.*

2. *Begin to do whatever it is that God wants you to do in order to please Him, regardless of whether you feel like it or not.*

3. *Deal biblically with any particular sin that may have triggered the bad feelings originally (although the feeling may not have originated in sin).*

4. *Avoid pity parties, blue funks, and gripe groups. Schedule your work, then follow your schedule—not your feelings.*

Please note, and this is important, I'm not presenting this information to help you solve a problem with depression. If you are experiencing depression, get help from a certified Biblical councilor (www.biblicalcounseling.com). Or at least get a copy of the Jay Adams booklet (www.prpbooks.com) so you can read the above list in its context. The point I'm making is that that depression is real, and the Biblical solution is nothing like what *Jesus Always* says.

As Christians we are not always filled with joy. But, the road back to joy is not the one described by the "Jesus" of *Jesus Always*. THIS IS IMPORTANT. What *Jesus Always* says about experiencing joy is not in agreement with what scripture says.

Let's look at a scriptural example. What was Paul's life like?

> ...*beaten times without number, often in danger of death. Five times I received from the Jews thirty-nine lashes. Three times I was beaten with rods, once I was stoned, three times I was shipwrecked, a night and a day I have spent in the deep. I have been on frequent journeys, in dangers from rivers, dangers from robbers, dangers from my countrymen, dangers from the Gentiles, dangers in the city, dangers in the wilderness, dangers on the sea, dangers among false brethren; I have been in labor and hardship, through many sleepless nights, in hunger and thirst, often without food, in cold and exposure. Apart from such external things, there is the daily pressure on me of concern for all the churches.* – 2 Corinthians 11:23b-28

With a job description like that, I don't think there would be many men willing to take on the work Paul did. He had a very tough time. Earlier in his second letter to the Corinthians he describes how he responded to all this:

> *We are afflicted in every way, but not crushed; perplexed, but not despairing; persecuted, but not forsaken; struck down, but not destroyed;* -- 2 Corinthians 4:8-9

In spite of all that happened to him, Paul was not despairing. Why? Let's continue reading in 2 Corinthians:

> *always carrying about in the body the dying of Jesus, so that the life of Jesus also may be manifested in our body.* – 2 Corinthians 4:10

There's the answer. The cross. Paul's eyes were always on the cross, the body of the dying of Jesus. In the words of the Helen Lemmel hymn:

> *O soul, are you weary and troubled?*
> *No light in the darkness you see?*
> *There's light for a look at the Savior,*
> *And life more abundant and free.*
>
> *Turn your eyes upon Jesus,*
> *Look full in His wonderful face,*

And the things of earth will grow strangely dim,
In the light of His glory and grace.

Through death into life everlasting
He passed, and we follow Him there;
O'er us sin no more hath dominion
For more than conqu'rors we are!

His Word shall not fail you, He promised;
Believe Him and all will be well;
Then go to a world that is dying,
His perfect salvation to tell!

Read these words carefully. They summarize the source of joy.

Notice that the focus is on the cross, which is the source of our hope. It does not say turn your eyes upon Jesus while he was preaching the Sermon on the Mount, or while he was raising Lazarus from the dead. The focus is on:

Through death into life everlasting
He passed, and we follow Him there;

The focus is on sin, that sin was defeated at the cross, and just as Jesus rose from the dead we will also rise from the dead and follow Him to glory.

We have joy when we repent, confess our sin, and have our eyes on eternity. Because of the cross we know our time here on earth is short and we'll spend eternity in glory with Jesus Christ. There is nothing anyone can do to take that away from you. The worst anyone can do is hurt you physically, but that is only momentary compared with eternity in heaven.

In summary, in the introduction to his commentary on Philippians, John MacArthur points out the six characteristics of joy: (The MacArthur New Testament Commentary, Philippians, 2001, pages 10 & 11)

> *1. Joy is a gift from God. David declared, "You have put gladness in my heart, more than when their grain and new wine abound. In peace I will*

both lie down and sleep, for You alone, O Lord, make me to dwell in safety." (Psalm 4:7-8)

2. God grants joy to those who believe the gospel. Jesus told his disciples, *"These things I have spoken to you so that My joy may be in you, and that you joy may be made full." (John 15:11)*

3. Joy is produced by God the Holy Spirit. *"For the kingdom of God is not eating and drinking, but righteousness and peace and joy in the Holy Spirit." (Roamns 14;17)*

4. Joy is experienced most fully as believers receive and obey God's Word. The prophet Jeremiah exulted, *"Your words were found and I ate them, and Your words became for me a joy and the delight of my heart." (Jeremiah 15:16)*

5. A believer's joy is deepened through trials. The full reality of joy is experienced when it is contrasted with sadness, sorrow and difficulties. *"You also have become imitators of us and of the Lord, having received the word in much tribulation with the joy of the Holy Spirit." (1 Thessalonians 1:6)*

6. A believer's joy is made complete when they set their hope on the glory of heaven. They are always to be *"rejoicing in hope." (Romans 12:12)*

Based on this list, if you are not experiencing joy, do you see where changes need to be made? Again it comes down to:

- You need to truly be a believer in Jesus Christ as your Savior. (Numbers 1, 2 & 3 on the list.)
- You need to receive and obey God's Word. This means reading your Bible, understanding it as it was originally written, and obeying it (getting sin out of your life). (Number 4 on the above list.)
- When you experience trials and difficult times, keep your eyes upon Jesus, the cross, and eternity. Be an imitator of Jesus and place your hope on the glory of heaven. This is how to

prevent trials from leading you into sin. (Number 5 & 6 on the list.)

This is nothing like what you find in *Jesus Always*. Instead, *Jesus Always* leads you away from the true Jesus of the Bible, and toward a false Jesus, a false gospel, and a false promise of salvation. The Bible leads you toward salvation and away from sin, and that is what produces true joy.

> [Paul] *was a larger-than-life model of a man of God whose joy never faltered. He resisted anything that threatened to come between him and his intimate fellowship and trust in the Lord. Paul certainly experienced sorrow and tears, suffered grief and disappointment, and was troubled by sinful, weak and contentious believers. Yet, there never seems to have been a time in his life as a believer when circumstances diminished his joy. In fact, it seems as it the worse affliction merely tightened his grip on salvation's joy.* – John MacArthur, New Testament Commentary, Philippians, 2001, page 56

None of what we've talked about concerning Biblical joy sounds anything like what *Jesus Calling* says. One of Sarah Young's favorite devotions, proves to be totally unbiblical. Don't let the unbiblical teaching of *Jesus Always* infect your life and your soul.

SHOULD YOU RUN FROM *JESUS ALWAYS*?

CHAPTER 16
JESUS SPEAKING:
SINFUL OR ACCEPTABLE?

I started out by saying that, if *Jesus Always* had not been written by putting the words of this devotion on the lips of Jesus, I would not have written this book. *Jesus Always* would just have been another poor quality, unbiblical devotional book… and there are a lot of those.

But *Jesus Always* is written as though Jesus is speaking, and we need to address the question: is this sinful or is it acceptable to God? Let's start by being sure we're all on the same page as far as definitions. We'll start by defining sin:

What Is Sin?

Sin is doing or thinking in a way that is contrary to how God acts and thinks. Righteousness is the opposite of sin. Righteousness is acting and thinking in accordance with the character of God. You are sinning any time you are not being righteous. So you are sinning whenever you act or think in a way contrary to how God acts or thinks. Why is this?

You were created in the image of God. When you do not reflect that image, you are sinning.

To help you know the character of God, He has given you His laws, such as the Ten Commandments. God's laws describe His character and what you should be like. If you break God's laws, you are sinning... meaning you are not behaving in a way that is consistent with God's character.

So, this is the question: is writing *Jesus Always* in a way such that "Jesus" is speaking the words of each devotion sinful or righteous? Is it acting in accordance with God's character or is it acting contrary to the character of God?

Let's take a look at the opening line of the January 2nd *Jesus Always* devotion. This is typical of all the *Jesus Always* devotions:[8]

> *"I AM YOUR JOY! These four words can light up your life. Since I am always with you, the joy of My Presence is continually accessible to you."* - Jesus Always, January 2nd

The *"I"* and *"My"* in the above quote refers to "Jesus." This is "Jesus" speaking.

Let's stop and think: Who is Jesus? He is God. When God speaks, and His words are recorded in writing, what are they called? That's an easy question, they are scripture.

Since the words in *Jesus Always* are represented as coming from the lips of the Son of God, then the book *"Jesus Always"* should be added to the Holy Bible. If we take it at face value, as it is written *Jesus Always* is an additional revelation from God. There is no question about this, because it is God who is represented as speaking.

But, the "About The Author" section in *Jesus Always* states:

> *Sarah Young's devotional writings are personal reflections from her daily quiet time of Bible reading, praying, and writing in prayer journals.* - Jesus Always, page 383

Sarah Young states that this is not Jesus speaking. These are just Sarah Young's "reflections." So there is no problem, right? But, the book is written as though Jesus was speaking. You can't have it both ways.

If this book were fiction, Jesus could be shown as speaking. I don't agree with that as being a good thing to do, but at least it would

---

19 – It's time to test what you've been learning. Do you see anything that is unbiblical in this quote? Is this quote promoting New Age beliefs? I hope your answer to both questions is "yes."

be identified as fiction. However, Sarah Young never represents *Jesus Always* as fiction. The *Jesus Always* devotions are presented as factual, giving instructions, training you with advice and commands that come from the lips of "Jesus." Putting these words in the mouth of Jesus makes them equivalent to scripture.

If Someone Is Represented As Saying Something They Never Said, What Is That Called?

It is lying. And that means *Jesus Always* is blasphemy. It is a lie to put words in on the lips of Jesus that he did not say.

As you've already seen, many of the words that have been put on the lips of our Savior in *Jesus Always* are not biblical. That represents "Jesus" Himself as a liar, because either the Holy Bible is wrong or the "Jesus" of *Jesus Always* is wrong. In both cases it is Jesus represented as speaking. One is telling the truth, and the other is a liar. That's a HUGE problem.

Jesus Always is blasphemy. Jesus never spoke the words Sarah Young is representing Him as saying. Christians know lying is wrong. We are to have the character of God, and lying is a major violation of God's character.

What Is Blasphemy?

Blasphemy is doing or saying something that does not show proper reverence for God. Blasphemy is also doing or saying anything that harms God's reputation... anything that detracts from His glory. Putting words into the mouth of Jesus, words Jesus never said, is misrepresenting God. Putting words in God's mouth, misrepresenting Biblical truth and promoting New Age theology, is a total misrepresentation of who God is. There is no question, that's blasphemy.

> *"Whenever anybody places words in the mouth of God that God did not say, they are misrepresenting Him as well. To write a book and present that book to others as the words of Jesus talking to them goes way beyond the standard practice of an author writing their thoughts and beliefs. They have taken their words and exalted them to the status of equality with the Bible no matter what claim they try to make otherwise."* - Robert Alan King, A Christian

SHOULD YOU RUN FROM *JESUS ALWAYS*?

Rebuttal to Sarah Young's Jesus Calling, Introduction, 2011 Kindle book

So Why Did Sarah Young Do This?

The only hint we have comes from Sarah Young's *Jesus Calling* book where she describes her motives:

> *"I have written from the perspective of Jesus speaking to help readers feel more personally connected with Him* [Jesus]" – Jesus Calling, 2014 10th Anniversary Edition, page XIII

In her words, the reason is so that you will feel more personally connected with Jesus. Can you become more personally connected with Jesus by reading something that misrepresents Jesus... something that has Jesus saying things He never said? No. You'd be reading a lie. Misrepresentation is a form of lying. Lying is a sin and sin doesn't bring you closer to Jesus. As we've seen, sin separates you from Jesus.

> *But your iniquities have made a separation between you and your God, and your sins have hidden His face from you so that He does not hear.* – Isaiah 59:2

Sarah Young is right in one respect. You can feel more personally connected with the "Jesus" of *Jesus Calling*. But, that does not mean you are growing closer to the real Jesus, the Son of God. The reality is you are *"becoming more personally connected to"* a lie. To a "Jesus" who does not exist. And that means you are moving further away from the real Jesus and closer to a false Jesus. Even a small lie moves you away from Jesus.

Yes, even a small lie about Jesus represents the almighty creator God as being less than who He is... less than the perfect, eternal, omniscient, holy, righteous, loving God we know from scripture. Never forget Jesus IS GOD. And never forget who God is.

> *For the LORD your God is God of gods and Lord of lords, the great, the mighty, and the awesome God.* - Deuteronomy 10:17

JESUS SPEAKING: SINFUL OR ACCEPTABLE

Here's another question: Does the "Jesus" of *Jesus Always* sound like the Jesus of the Bible? Read the book of Isaiah starting with chapter 40. This is the true Jesus speaking:

> *Listen to Me, O Jacob, even Israel whom I called; I am He, I am the first, I am also the last. Surely My hand founded the earth, And My right hand spread out the heavens; besides Me there is no God.* - Isaiah 48:12-13

Who is speaking here? The Son of God, Jesus. These words, as well as most of Isaiah chapters 40 through 66, are a direct quotes from Jesus. They are the words of the Son of God. How do we know this is Jesus speaking? Go to Isaiah 48:16

> *Come near to Me, listen to this: From the first I have not spoken in secret, From the time it took place, I was there.* **And now the Lord GOD has sent Me, and His Spirit.**

Who did the sending? "The Lord God," the Father.

Who was sent? The speaker, "Me." That can only be the Son. The One who has been speaking since the beginning of chapter 40.

Who was also sent? The Spirit.

Here in the Old Testament we see the Trinity. The Father is doing the sending. It is the Son who has been speaking since chapter 40. And the Spirit was also sent. These are the words of Jesus Christ, the Son of God. This is what the true Jesus Christ sounds like. His words have a depth and richness not found in *Jesus Always*. This is not the Jesus of the *Jesus Always* devotional book.

Never forget Jesus IS GOD. You do not become more personally connected to God through words placed in His mouth by a human writer... words He never said... words that in many cases contradict what the real Jesus has said in the Bible. Any form of a lie is sin, and sin separates us from God.

The *Jesus Always* devotions DO NOT honor or glorify God, nor do they correctly represent the character of God.

CHAPTER 17
BUT, JESUS SPEAKING MAKES THE BOOK MORE INTERESTING

Several people who like Sarah Young's first book, *Jesus Calling*, have told me: *"It's no big deal. It's just a point of view. Having Jesus speak the words in Jesus Calling helps make the book more interesting."*

To say this is to forget who we are talking about... God. It is a big deal. Does God lend His name to be used for a product endorsement? Does God want His name used in a book just so that book will be more interesting? No, never!

You cannot buy or borrow the name of God to help make a book, a movie, a theme park, or anything else more interesting. God is not some famous movie star, TV pitchman, or flim-flam man willing to have his name attached to any book or product someone wishes to sell. God is holy. Only what is of God, may be attributed to God.

Never Forget Who God Is

As for God, His way is perfect; The word of the LORD is proven; - 2 Samuel 22:31 (NKJV)

Thus says the Lord, your Redeemer, and the one who formed you from the womb, "I, the Lord, am the maker of all things, Stretching out the heavens by Myself and spreading out the earth all alone, Causing the omens of boasters to fail, Making fools out of diviners, Causing wise men to draw back And turning their knowledge into foolishness." – Jesus speaking in Isaiah 44:24-25

Let's think about this. What is accomplished by writing a devotional book from the point of view of Jesus (God)? It gives authority to what is said. Authority it does not deserve, since these are not actually the words of Jesus.

Without regard to what the author may have intended, many readers are left with the impression that Jesus is speaking to them personally through this devotional book. The words of Jesus have authority... Jesus is God. And for that reason, only the actual words of Jesus... the words of scripture... should ever be attributed as coming from Jesus.

Sarah Young is not just writing from any point of view, let's say the point of view of a famous pastor. She is writing from the point of view of God. No one should do that, unless they are writing the inspired word of God... in other words unless it is scripture. Otherwise, what is written is deceptive. Why? Because, coming from God's lips, it appears to have authority and trustworthiness that, in reality, it doesn't have.

> *While she acknowledges that "I knew these writings were not inspired as Scripture is" (xii), she still desired "to share some of the messages I have received" (xiii). There is simply no way around it: Sarah Young is claiming to have received these messages directly from God. Whether or not you formally place those messages in the same category of Scripture, she is claiming to be a modern prophetess, receiving the Lord's word and transmitting it to others.*
>
> *Friends, this is dangerous. We cannot say "thus saith the Lord" without considering the incredible weight of that responsibility, the closed canon of Scripture, and the fearful judgment promised to those who falsely claim to speak for God and/or add to His Word."* – Rick Thomas' Review of *Jesus Calling* (http://tiny.cc/ocsz4x)

You Can't Say It Is Wrong. Her Intentions Were Good.

Some of the people I've discussed *Jesus Calling* with have responded, *"But her [Sarah Young] intentions are good."*

Jesus does not judge based on intentions. We can be Christians with good intentions and still be teaching falsehoods. In the Sermon on the Mount Jesus reveals that even believers can disobey God, and teach others to do the same.

> *Whoever then annuls one of the least of these commandments, and teaches others to do the same, shall be called least in the kingdom of heaven;* - Matthew 5:19

Notice that the penalty the false teacher receives is to be *"called least in the kingdom of heaven."* That means Jesus is talking about someone who is saved. They are in the kingdom, so they are a believer. But, they are teaching people to violate God's commandments. They are probably very sincere about what they are teaching, but it is still false teaching.

So we see from scripture that even true believers can present false teaching... lies... and they can be very sincere in their teaching. Does that make the false teaching acceptable? No. The good intentions of the teacher make no difference. If what is written is false, the good intentions of an author make no difference. You can be very sincere, and be very wrong.

What is written in *Jesus Always* are not the words of Jesus. This is God we are talking about! God does not lend His name to be used to make a book more interesting. Any book that puts words in the mouth of God (Jesus), other than the words of scripture, is giving those words authority they do not deserve. That is very dangerous, and it makes this a book a book no Christians should be reading.

CHAPTER 18
BUT, *JESUS ALWAYS* REALLY HELPED ME

When talking with people about Sarah Young's previous book, *Jesus Calling*, the number one reason people gave me for liking it was because it helped them have a good start to their day. You also see this in the reviews people write on Amazon:

There is nothing wrong with something that helps you to feel better, as long as it is Biblical. God has given us feelings, and there is a purpose for our feelings. But, we need to be sure we are getting this help from a Biblical source.

New Age practices and spirituality do have real power, and can result in feelings of peace and joy. But, the sources of those feelings and experiences are demonic. Demons have no problem helping us to feel good, if it takes our focus off Christ.

> *Remember there is a beautiful side of evil—deceptive, subtle, adorned with all manner of spiritual refinements, but no less from the pit of hell than that which is blatantly demonic.* - Johanna Michaelsen, The Beautiful Side of Evil, 1975, page216

When looking at how they impact us, one of the differences between the Bible and *Jesus Always* is that scripture deals with knowledge, understanding, and the promises of God. *Jesus Always* primarily deals with experiences, feelings, and emotions.

Although there are a few calls to read scripture, the overall approach of *Jesus Always* is to manipulate your emotions. It's a book that makes you feel good because it places you and your feelings at the center. The Jesus of *Jesus Always* exists to serve you. That's a huge simplification, but that's what *Jesus Always* is about… feelings and manipulating your emotions.

Why do people read *Jesus Always*? Because it makes them feel good. Because the focus is on them and their feelings. *Jesus Always* is a book about YOU. On the other hand scripture is about GOD. Scripture gives you a growing knowledge of God and His will. That is where you find truth and true healing. In his prayer for the Colossian church Paul shows us what the answer should be:

> *We have not ceased to pray for you and to ask that you may be filled with the knowledge of His will in all spiritual wisdom and understanding.* – Colossians 1:9

Paul never prays for believers to feel good, or have a good start to their day. Paul prays that believers be filled with the knowledge of God.

If you are reading *Jesus Always* because it makes you feel good, your focus is in the wrong place. It is on YOU, instead of on GOD. It's a focus on making YOU feel good, not on growing closer to God through knowing Him better. Paul's prayer was for growing knowledge, not for the Colossians to have fuzzy-warm, comfortable feelings.

What is scripture about? God. Scripture focuses on God. It focuses on giving you knowledge about God… on what He has done, and on His plan for restoration and redemption. Does reading scripture result in feeling good? Yes, it does. But, that's not the purpose of scripture. It's the result of reading scripture… the result of learning about God, what He has done, and His promises.

> *Therefore we do not lose heart, but though our outer man is decaying, yet our inner man is being renewed day by day. For momentary, light affliction is producing for us an eternal weight of glory far beyond all comparison, while we look not at the things which are seen, but at the things which are not seen; for the things which are seen are temporal, but the things which are not seen are eternal.*- 2 Corinthians 4:16-18

How do we get knowledge about Jesus? It's very simple, read the scriptures. Desire God and read His word.

Truth: Focuses On God.

Falsehood: Focuses On The Results Of Knowing God (On What You Get).

Knowing God fills us with joy! Why are we filled with joy? Because, knowing Jesus as our Savior means we are children of God and joint heirs with Christ, as Paul describes in Romans:

> *For as many as are led by the Spirit of God, these are sons of God. For you did not receive the spirit of bondage again to fear, but you received the Spirit of adoption by whom we cry out, "Abba, Father." The Spirit Himself bears witness with our spirit that we are children of God, and if children, then heirs; heirs of God and joint heirs with Christ, if indeed we suffer with Him, that we may also be glorified together. For I consider that the sufferings of this present time are not worthy to be compared with the glory which shall be revealed in us. For the earnest expectation of the creation eagerly waits for the revealing of the sons of God.* - Romans 8:14-19

Where is Paul's focus? On God. As you read the above, what is it that we have done? Nothing. Why should we have joy when we are suffering? Because of God and His promise of eternal life. Because any suffering we experience now is nothing compared with partaking of the glory of God as an adopted child of God.

> *"A final truth about adoption is that it involves an inheritance....How unexpected and how breathtaking is the gracious provision of God! The marvel increases with the news that we are co-heirs with Christ. Sharing His sufferings may be looked at as simply the cost of discipleship. Yet it has a brighter aspect, because it is the prelude to partaking with Him of the coming glory."* – Everett F. Harrison, Expositors Bible Commentary, 1986, Romans, page 93.

Does this focus on knowledge make the Bible seem rather dry and impersonal? Isn't God about relationships? Yes, He is. Have you noticed that in the Bible knowledge implies a relationship?

For the Christian, knowledge implies a relationship. For example, when the Bible says that "Adam knew Eve his wife" (Genesis 4:1, NKJV), it means he had a physical union with her. Spiritual relationships are also described this way. Jesus used the word know to refer to His saving relationship with those who follow Him: "I am the good shepherd; I know my sheep and my sheep know me" (John 10:14). He also told His disciples, "You will know the truth, and the truth will set you free" (John 8:32). By contrast, Jesus said to the unbelieving Jews, "You do not know [my Father]" (verse 55). Therefore, to know Christ is to have faith in Him, to follow Him, to have a relationship with Him, to love and be loved by Him. (See also John 14:7; 1 Corinthians 8:3; Galatians 4:9; and 2 Timothy 2:19.) Increasing in the knowledge of God is part of Christian maturity and is something all Christians are to experience as we "grow in the grace and knowledge of our Lord and Savior Jesus Christ" (2 Peter 3:18). – Got Questions Ministry, http://tiny.cc/7uhb5x

BUT, *Jesus* Always Helped Me!
If a Book "Helps" You, Does That Make It A Good Book?

Reading a novel such as *A Tale of Two Cities* has helped some people get through a tough time. However, whether or not a book has "helped" you is not the criteria you should use to judge that book. There are web sites that recommend reading the Satanic Bible because some people feel it has helped them. Does that mean the Satanic Bible is a good book? No!

Muslims talk about how the Quran has changed their lives for the good. Does that mean the Quran is a good book? No!

The criteria is: does it conform to scripture? Is it fully in agreement with scripture? Only in scripture will you find the answers that truly help you. It's amazing, scripture really does have the answers to all of our problems and troubles.

What then shall we say to these things? If God is for us, who is against us? He who did not spare His own Son, but delivered Him over for us all, how will He not also with Him freely give us all things? – Romans 8:31-32

What about emotional healing? Does the Bible have any answers? What does scripture say about healing when you are experiencing fear, anxiety, and depression? Can it help you overcome addictions?

The Bible has the healing answer for each of these, as well as every other emotional problem you could have. Yes, some problems are physical. If you are anxious and can't sleep, it may be because you've had 20 cups of coffee today. But, scripture does have the answers for every emotional problem. You will find the general principle in Ephesians chapter four:

> *So this I say, and affirm together with the Lord, that you walk no longer just as the Gentiles also walk, in the futility of their mind, being darkened in their understanding, excluded from the life of God because of the ignorance that is in them, because of the hardness of their heart; and they, having become callous, have given themselves over to sensuality or the practice of every kind of impurity with greediness.*
>
> *But you did not learn Christ in this way, if indeed you have heard Him and have been taught in Him, just as truth is in Jesus, that, in reference to your former manner of life, you lay aside the old self, which is being corrupted in accordance with the lusts of deceit, and that you be renewed in the spirit of your mind, and put on the new self, which in the likeness of God has been created in righteousness and holiness of the truth.* - Ephesians 4:17-24

These verses in Ephesians tell us exactly what we need to do. What is it? To paraphrase the above: lay aside the old self and put on the new self. We are to get rid of the old self that is experiencing depression, or fear, or anger, or even a bad habit... and that is where most people stop. They do something to get rid of the problem, and then say, "The problem is fixed. It's gone." But, if you don't replace the old self with something else, the old self comes right back.

When you get rid of something it leaves a vacuum waiting to be filled. If you don't fill it with something Biblical... the old self just comes right back.

The principle is to get rid of the old, and replace it with the new, Biblical self. Does *Jesus Always* say anything like this? Let's find out. The idea of putting off the old and putting on the new is expressed in three devotions.

This involves putting off your old self—your old way of thinking and doing things—and putting on the new self. – *Jesus Always*, June 24th

You need to be made new in the attitude of your mind and to put on the new self—becoming increasingly godly, righteous, and holy. – *Jesus Always*, March 27th

These sound Biblical. BUT, the question you need to ask is: what is the "new self" that you are supposed to put on? Is it the image of Jesus Christ as described in scripture, or is it something or someone else? The answer is given in the May 7th devotion.

Until then, I am training you to be made new in the attitude of your mind, to put on the new self. – *Jesus Always*, May 7th

Although your new self is being conformed to My image, this process doesn't erase the essence of who you are. – *Jesus Always*, May 7th

Jesus Always wants you to be conformed to the image of the fictional "Jesus" of *Jesus Always*. A "Jesus" who is deeply involved in New Age (unbiblical) practices such as Practicing the Presence. That's deception. What *Jesus Always* is saying sounds Biblical, but it is leading you to be conformed to the image of demons. RUN!

> Do you need to find a good Biblical counselor? Many counselors say they are "Biblical," but that does not mean they base their counseling on scripture. Look for a counselor who is certified by the Association of Certified Biblical Counselors (ACBC). More information is available on their web site: *www.biblicalcounseling.com*

CHAPTER 19
TRUSTING THE
REAL JESUS TO HEAL YOU

You're having a bad day, you missed breakfast and lunch, you've hurt your arm and need some help changing a flat tire on your car. A man stops and offers to help. He's well dressed and is full of advice, not only for changing tires, but on how to maintain your car. You talk for about 15 minutes and you find you are enjoying the conversation. Your day doesn't seem so bad after all. You've met a nice guy, who is pleasant to talk with, and he's promised to help you.

As he's talking the man picks up the jack… and slides it under the car… that's progress. Then he pats the flat tire and assures you it will be just fine… you just need to relax and let him take care of it.

You're feeling a little better. But, an hour later, although he did take the spare out of the trunk, the tire still hasn't been changed. This is the Jesus of *Jesus Always*. You get promises. You get a dash of truth. And you feel better for a while. But you are trusting someone who cannot deliver on the promises he's made. The tire never gets changed.

The Bible tells us to trust Jesus… the real Jesus and the actual words of scripture. And… this is important… we are to trust him in a very different way than *Jesus Always* asks us to trust. The key question we'll look at in this chapter is: what are we to trust Jesus for?

SHOULD YOU RUN FROM *JESUS ALWAYS*?

Trusting the Jesus of *Jesus Always*

I picked a random date. Then I looked at the next ten days of devotions and wrote down the benefits *Jesus Always* seems to identify as a result of trusting Jesus, or being in the Presence of "Jesus". I've tried to stay with a literal reading, however it is easy to interpret *Jesus Always* in many different ways. So if you repeat what I've done, you may get a slightly different result.

Here is the list of the benefits of trusting Jesus, based on ten days in April. According to *Jesus Always* you are to trust Jesus to:

- get you safely through the day (April 6th)
- keep you from being separated from him (April 7th)
- steady you in your ups and downs through the day (April 8th)
- guide you along the pathway of life (April 9th)
- sustain you (April 10th)
- take you to Glory—to be with Him forever (April 10th)
- transform the way you think (April 11th h)
- make you ready for anything (April 12th)
- bring you success (April 13th)
- keep your feet on the path of Peace (April 14th)
- find spiritual and emotional security (April 14th)
- be your God Friend taking care of you (April 15th)

To summarize the above, I'd say that Jesus' primary goal is for you to have a good day. If you trust him, he'll guide you through the day, keeping you safe, eliminating troubles, and giving you strength and peace. And, by the way, in the end he'll take you to glory.

My impression, from reading all of the *Jesus Always* devotions, is that to trust means to relax in his Presence. You need to cultivate an attitude of quietness and calmness and live in the now... don't be thinking about yesterday or tomorrow. When you feel like you are experiencing his Presence, he will guide you and help you deal with whatever comes up. The promised result is Peace and Joy (capitalized). I don't know if you noticed, but this is straight out of the box New Age doctrine.

Yes, *Jesus Always* does include many Biblical words, phrases, and principles. April 10th promises that someday "Jesus" will *"take you to*

Glory to be with him forever." That sounds biblical, although if you read the devotion almost everything leading up to that promise is New Age spirituality mixed with Christian phrases. The "Glory" *Jesus Always* is talking about is not the same as what scripture talks about.

Trusting the Jesus of the Bible

Trust in the LORD *with all your heart, and do not lean on your own understanding.* - Proverbs 3:5

What's important is what scripture says. In scripture, what does it mean to trust the Jesus of the Holy Bible? It means you can trust His character. You can trust His wisdom, His power, His faithfulness, and His goodness. You can trust that what He tells you to do is the right thing to do. All of this means you can trust His promises. For example, Jesus has promised that if you believe in Him, you will not perish:

For God so loved the world, that He gave His only begotten Son, that whoever believes in Him shall not perish, but have eternal life. - John 3:16

This is a promise of salvation. Believers are promised eternal life. Jesus is saying that if you trust Him, you will not experience the second death—the lake of fire—but will experience eternal life in God's presence in heaven forever. What a wonderful promise!

Jesus Always Says The Same Thing, What's Wrong?

How do you know you can trust the Jesus of the Bible? Because He never did anything to betray your trust. Even His most fantastic promise, that there is life after death, was verified by His resurrection. The true Jesus has never lied to you, He has never lead you away from truth, and His focus is always where it should be, on glorifying God.

The "Jesus" of *Jesus Always* cannot say the same thing. As you've seen in this book, this false "Jesus" misleads you about the meaning of scripture. He misrepresents the character of God, taking away the Father's glory. Instead of leading you to truth, he leads you into unbiblical New Age spiritual practices such as the Presence, silencing your thoughts, and being in the "now." And he bribes you and manipulates you by putting the focus of these devotions on you, instead of on Him where it belongs.

The real Jesus is perfect. Human and demonic creations are flawed, and you can see those flaws in the "Jesus" of *Jesus Always.* Don't follow a false Jesus, a "Jesus" you cannot trust, and who is leading you down the wide road away from the true Jesus Christ.

CHAPTER 20
SHOULD YOU RUN FROM JESUS ALWAYS?

The key question is: should you RUN from *Jesus Always*? I hope you've seen the answer is, YES. *Jesus Always* is not a Biblical devotional. Do as scripture commands RUN (Psalm 37:27). Resist the devil… and he will flee from you. (James 4:7)

Why?

- *Jesus Always* misrepresents scripture. In every example we looked at, *Jesus Always* gets something wrong about scripture. From having a wrong understanding of scripture, to misrepresenting the path to joy in one of Sarah Young's favorite devotions. *Jesus Always* is not a Biblical devotional. This alone is enough reason to throw away your copy of *Jesus Always*.

- *Jesus Always* shows no understanding of the foundational principle that sin separates us from God and is the source of problems such as fear, anxiety, and depression. Sin is not talked about as separating us from God, nor is sin identified as the root cause of the problems we all have. (Note: this is consistent with New Age beliefs about sin, but it is not consistent with what the Bible teaches.)

- *Jesus Always* teaches New Age principles and practices. This is most easily seen in the capitalization of words such as Joy,

Peace and Glory, and the use of phrases such as Glory-strength and "holy illumination." This type of capitalization and word usage indicates a belief that god is everything, and everything is god. It is the belief in the oneness with god and it leads to the belief in the Presence of god within you. Since god is within you, you can communicate with him using techniques such as quieting yourself (silence), being in the now, and saying "breath prayers." These are prayers that repeat words or short phrases, sometimes whispering them. All of these New Age beliefs and practices are characteristic of the devotions in *Jesus Always*.

New Age teaching is also seen in the emphasis on coming into the Presence of Jesus. By itself, the New Age teaching in *Jesus Always* is sufficient reason to never pick up this devotional.

- Jesus is speaking in *Jesus Always*. As we saw, if you did this with Oprah you'd quickly be sued. God is holy, righteous, majestic, and the most high. Why do we think we can do to God what we cannot do to a human television personality? To put words in the mouth of God, that He didn't say, is blasphemous. To put words in His mouth that contradict and misrepresent scripture, and that promote unbiblical New Age beliefs and practices... means that *Jesus Always* is putting heresy, anti-Christian teaching, lies, and other blasphemies on the lips of Jesus. That is total unacceptable.

- Jesus came to seek and save the lost. Everything He said and did was focused on this objective. This includes numerous warnings not to be deceived by false teaching and false teachers, as well as warning people who think they were saved but who are not (false converts). We also saw that warning against false doctrine is emphasized more than anything else in the New Testament, even more than love and unity. So these warning are incredibly important.

Jesus' focus on salvation is nowhere seen in *Jesus Always*. In addition, *Jesus Always* has the characteristic that is the most common characteristic of false teaching: a total disregard for discernment, and a lack of warnings about false teaching and false converts.

The evidence is overwhelming... *Jesus Always* is not a Christian devotional. It is a New Age/New Spirituality book that leads people away from the true Jesus of scripture. Each of the above points, by themselves, is reason enough to reject *Jesus Always*. If you have a copy of *Jesus Always* or *Jesus Calling*, throw it away. Don't ever give it as a gift and do not keep a copy in your home. YES, you should RUN from *Jesus Always*, just as the Apostle John ran from the false teacher Cerinthus.

SHOULD YOU RUN FROM *JESUS ALWAYS*?

ABOUT THE AUTHOR

Steve Hudgik served as the pastor of the Cannon Beach Bible Church, in Cannon Beach, Oregon from 2013 until September 2018, and then as an associate pastor until October 2019.

Steve has been the executive director of the Move to Assurance (MTA) ministry since 2000. MTA is involved in evangelism, outreach, and apologetics ministries. Some of the MTA web sites include:

www.911Christ.com
www.MTAbible.com
www.MoveToAssurance.org
www.SciencePastor.com
www.DinosaursForJesus.com

**Other books by Steve Hudgik
are available on Amazon.com**

OTHER CHRISTIAN BOOKS BY STEVE HUDGIK

Did God Really Say?
Answering humanist attacks on the bible.
Steve goes to the American Humanist web site and answers every accusation and attack they make against scripture and the Bible.

Mrs. Bartlett and Her Class at the Metropolitan Tabernacle
Written by her son Edward (with notes and annotations by Steve), this is the amazing true story about a prayer warrior and evangelist in Charles Spurgeon's church.

The Presence of God
A commentary on the book of Esther
Esther is the only book in the bible that does not mention God, yet God's presence can be seen throughout this book

RUN! It's Jesus Calling
Pastor Steve examine Sarah Young's first devotional, comparing it with scripture. The result is that we see that "Jesus Calling" falls far short of the truth of God's word.

Happy Are The...
Discovering joy through the beatitudes

All of Steve's books are available on Amazon

Printed in Great Britain
by Amazon